IMAGES
of America

STEPHENVILLE

This 1856 survey map of Erath County depicts the fledgling town of Stephenville, located along the banks of the Bosque River. John Blair, a Missourian who fell at the Alamo, posthumously received a tract straddling the river. His heirs sold the acreage to John M. Stephen, who created the town site that was surveyed by George B. Erath and his helpers, as pictured on page 12. (Texas General Land Office.)

ON THE COVER: From the establishment of Stephenville, religion has played an integral part in community members' lives. In the early 1900s, traveling ministers spoke to packed "houses" (they were technically tabernacles) at outdoor meetings. Although the 21st-century venue has changed, today many Stephenville residents remain very devoted and enthusiastic about their faiths. (Stephenville Historical Museum.)

IMAGES
of America

STEPHENVILLE

Ricky L. Sherrod

ARCADIA
PUBLISHING

Published by Arcadia Publishing
Charleston, South Carolina

Library of Congress Control Number: 2010936556

For all general information, please contact Arcadia Publishing:
Telephone 843-853-2070
Fax 843-853-0044
E-mail sales@arcadiapublishing.com
For customer service and orders:
Toll-Free 1-888-313-2665

Visit us on the Internet at www.arcadiapublishing.com

*To Stephenville's youth—to each coming generation that will write
its own new chapter in the story of the "City of Champions"*

CONTENTS

ACKNOWLEDGMENTS

The success of any volume like this rests on a historically sensitive community willing to share collective resources. Happily, Stephenville's citizens and organizations contributed enthusiastically. Stephenville Historical Museum (SHM) and the Dick Smith Library Cross Timbers Historical Image Project (CTHI) of Tarleton State University (TSU) provided most of the images on the following pages. Images without courtesy lines were supplied by SHM, chaired by Robin Ritchie.

Other institutions and organizations lending support to this project included Stephenville Independent School District (SISD); Stephenville Chamber of Commerce (July Danley, president and chief executive officer, and Courtney Vanden Berge, marketing and events director); the Stephenville *Empire-Tribune* (Sara Vanden Berge, managing editor; Amanda Jenkins-Kimble, staff writer; and Brad Keith, sports editor); and the Erath County Historical Commission (ECHC—Cathey Hartmann, chairperson). Without such backing, this book would not have been possible.

No one gave material and moral support as enthusiastically or unselfishly as my Stephenville High School (SHS) colleague Debbie Wesson Cashell. She donated untold hours of volunteer service, taking pictures, doing research on local history, and donating invaluable family images. Debbie and her husband, SHS coach Yancey Cashell, have my unqualified gratitude.

I would like to thank the Allens—Scott and Jenny and Brad and Nancy (ECHC chairperson, 1999–2006)—who aided greatly by contributing multiple unique images. Nancy's generous sharing of personal files was a turning point that brought the project to critical mass. Glenda Stone (assistant director of monographs and technical services of Dick Smith Library) came repeatedly to my rescue, as she has on innumerable occasions before our collaboration on *Stephenville*. She went above and beyond, locating and scanning many of the CTHI images in this volume.

On their shifts of volunteer service, author and retired teacher Sherri Knight and Huckabay teacher Cindy Shipman made the SHM's photograph collection easily accessible. M. Wayne Sherrod contributed greatly, allowing use of his personal historical photograph collection. Wayne's encyclopedic knowledge of Stephenville's architectural history was an invaluable asset. The following work colleagues also smoothed my pathway: SISD superintendent Dr. Darrell Floyd and his administrative assistant Norma Cervetto gave me free run of the school district's historical files and documents; SHS principal Travis Stilwell enthusiastically encouraged this project and approved my attendance at the 2010 Texas State Historical Association meeting in Dallas where the book was conceived; and my friends, coaches Joseph Gillespie and Michael Copeland, helped document the rich successes of Yellow Jacket and Honey Bee athletic history. T. J. Steed—with his dad, Steve, the creator of the "Can Fan"—guided me through a 21st-century technological wilderness, leading me to marginal, but functional, competence in using modern scanners.

Local authors, writers, and Erath County historians Sherri Knight, Wayne Sherrod, Cindy Shipman, Glenda Stone, Joyce Whitis, and Dan Young all examined my manuscript and captions at various stages of preparation. So did TSU history professor Christopher Guthrie. Collectively, they prevented numerous factual errors. For their help, I am sincerely grateful. I am solely accountable for the mistakes that remain.

I am also grateful to my wife, Annette, who pleasantly endured as a "writer's widow" during the summer months of this volume's preparation. Thanks as well to Marshall Sherrod, whose financial donations for considerable sundry expenses may ultimately save the author from running too deeply into the red.

Finally, thanks to Arcadia's Luke Cunningham, who helped at the project's inception, and to Winnie Rodgers, who stepped in soon thereafter and guided me successfully to the finish line.

INTRODUCTION

At first glance, little suggests a connection between the Cross Timbers Texas town of Stephenville and the holiest of Texas shrines, San Antonio's Alamo, located 260 miles due south.

Stephenville was not even surveyed until 1855. Draftsman Joseph Martin's 1856 Erath County map reveals a sizable tract straddling the Bosque River, a tract where today's city stands. Upon that acreage, "heirs of John Blair" is inscribed.

On March 6, 1836, according to *Erath County Deed Book B*, page 185, 33-year-old Blair was among those "killed in the Alamo . . . with Colonel Travis in the defense of Texas." Blair's participation in the Texas Revolution entitled him to an ample land grant in the newly established Lone Star Republic, a grant comprising 17 and 2/3 labors of land (3,127 acres). Part of that reward was "on the main Bosque in the Cross Timbers," the future site of Stephenville. On February 24, 1853, in McLennan County's Waco, John M. Stephen paid $445.49 to the brother of the deceased and attorney Thomas Miligan Blair for that Bosque River tract.

Stephen's purchase placed him literally at the end of the Texas frontier. In his *Memoirs*, George Bernard Erath—Austrian-born immigrant, Native American fighter, soldier at San Jacinto, surveyor, and Texas congressman—declared "this settlement was the farthest west of any on the waters of the Brazos." In *Grand Ol' Erath*, a 20th-century Erath County state congressman, H. Grady Perry reflected, "one wonders just what brought the first settlers here . . . There were very few natural advantages or resources in the county." In fact, the first pioneers encountered a luxuriant ecology with waist-high grasslands that distinguished the region until the first decade of the 20th century, by which time consolidation of small farms into big ranches altered the area's original environment.

Stephen's Scots-Irish ancestors typically settled at the edge of what they perceived as unused. Most Scots-Irish immigrants who came to the United States between 1765 and 1775 settled in Virginia's backcountry far west of established communities in the Virginia Tidewater. Stephen's ancestors did not remain there long. The family's migratory trail followed that of the westward -moving American frontiersmen's path, which went as follows: first to trans-Appalachia, Kentucky; next to Missouri, which was where John M. Stephen was born in 1814; and then to Southern Arkansas, which was where John's brother William was born in 1828. Arkansas was a well-used staging ground for ambitious frontier-loving migrants intending to exploit fertile Louisiana or Texas river valleys where cotton fortunes could be made.

In March 1831, John's father, James Stephen, received a sizable grant within the Austin Colony. By the 1850s, both father and son lived near the Brazos River, at which time John purchased land where a town was soon named after him. Paperwork transferring the Blair grant to Stephen bears the significant witness signature of George Erath. Stephen and Erath worked hand in glove to create a new population center on this fringe of settlement in 1854 Texas.

In May 1855, Erath led 30 settlers who put down roots in what became the Texas county that eventually bore his name. The group included John M. Stephen and his brother William Franklin Stephen. On the Fourth of July, 1855, these pioneer-settler-surveyors completed the mapping of Stephenville's town square. In 1856, the Sixth Texas Legislature carved Erath County from Bosque and Coryell Counties. Residents christened the newly established population center "Stephenville" after the man donating land for the city. Stephen's considerable assets well enabled him to donate on his specific terms, which meant the city had to be named in his honor and also designated the county seat.

Stephen subsequently prospered. In 1850, this 34-year-old Missouri-born farmer declared $15,000 in real estate and held two slaves. In 1860, four years after the creation of Stephenville and Erath County, he identified himself as a "planter" with $25,000 in real estate and $30,000 in personal estate. The latter reflected 15 slaves, making him the second largest Erath County holder of bondsmen. With four slave cabins, Stephen owned more slave housing than any other county resident, as recorded in the 1860 federal census. Meanwhile, the county developed quickly.

The initial wave of settlers introduced basic rudiments of Anglo-Celtic civilization. Thomas Arendell erected the first of many log houses, the standard form of construction for early city dwellers. The Stephen brothers established the town's first store in 1854. The first local election occurred on August 4, 1856; the first tax roll came the following year. In July 1857, John M. Stephen became Stephenville's first postmaster. By 1858, Erath County's population was 766. By 1859, Stephenville boasted a hotel that was regularly frequented by the buffalo hunters pursuing American bison, which, as late as the mid-1870s, grazed within 3 miles of town. In 1860, the town of Stephenville had 120 residents. To bring order and organization to the frontier, pioneers built a courthouse, which became the repository of paperwork constituting the city's historical memory, the collective community consciousness, and a place housing documentation for personal private property. The growth of Stephenville slowed during the Civil War, but during Reconstruction, Erath County's population increased, as southerners from across the defeated Confederacy looked for a fresh start on the "Lone Star State's" periphery. By 1871, Stephenville's population had grown to 300.

Economic opportunity fueled Stephenville's expansion. The original pioneers risked their future on a move to make a fortune in cattle, cotton, or both. John M. Stephen was among a cast of thousands who, since Eli Whitney's 1793 invention of the gin, migrated regularly in search of fertile, inexpensive agricultural acreage. By 1860, Stephen's $55,000 in total assets—$1.46 million in today's economy—made him Erath County's wealthiest resident. Like a host of other Texas-bound migrants, he aspired to plant cotton. However, hopes of 1850s cotton planters, overspreading West Central Texas, came to naught. The Civil War and emancipation reconfigured possibilities. Even before the war, the modest potential of the Bosque as a watery transportation artery for cotton and, more importantly, the palpable absence of an Erath County cotton gin forced most residents of the newly forming county to choose different agricultural options.

During the war and early Reconstruction, economic activity slowed dramatically. Cotton planting temporarily lost appeal. Even before the war, the principal profitable Erath County pursuit was not yet cotton production. In 1860, a total of 251 residents of Erath County identified themselves as farmers. Another 165 described themselves as stock farmers or stock ranchers. There were almost 100 more farmers than cattle raisers, but as a group, the latter were far more wealthy. Cattle ranchers were far more likely to hold assets into the multiple thousands of dollars. From the days of original settlement to today, Erath County enjoys ample black, chocolate loam topsoil that produces abundant grasslands, which, in turn, provides excellent grazing for livestock. In the 1850s, land was available and inexpensive. Thus, raising cattle became Erath County's most lucrative economic pursuit from the end of the war until the first cotton gin's arrival in the 1870s. The first gins dramatically altered the local economy.

A paltry 57 bales constituted Erath County's 1860 cotton crop. By 1870, production rose only to 167. Cotton nevertheless became the county's major crop for 40 years, from 1875 to 1915, supplanting cattle as the staple of economic life between 1870 and 1890, years during which the county's cattle count dropped 75 percent. Cotton enjoyed a meteoric rise, becoming the money crop and backbone of the economy. As cotton increased, so did the county population. Farmers concentrated on the fleecy fiber, resurrecting cotton's antebellum royal status, and produced 2,847 bales in 1880. By 1890, production was 17,390 bales. Cotton ruled again as king.

Initially, farm to market cotton transportation was difficult and expensive. Cotton's success was largely the result of the railroad's arrival in Erath County's Alexander (1881) and Dublin (about 1882). The Fort Worth and Rio Grande Railroad reached Stephenville in fall 1889. Incentive to grow cotton also increased in 1894 with the establishment of Stephenville's cotton oil mill. Figures from 1900 reveal 24,852 ginned bales produced by 50 Erath County gins. A decade later, that figure climbed to 57,673. Production in 1910 coincided with Erath County's peak in population, totaling 32,095 residents. Cotton production dropped over the coming years; so did county population. The 1920 and 1930 federal censuses lists 28,585 and 20,804 respectively.

The dethroning of Erath County cotton was partly a function of the blind economic force of supply and demand. As cotton production expanded, cotton prices fell, equipment cost increased, and taxes remained the same. Farmers had less incentive to produce. If price decline failed to strike a final knockout punch, the cotton economy could not contend with the double-blow dealt by the Mexican boll weevil, which reached Texas by the beginning of the 20th century, and soil exhaustion that was produced by years of poor conservation habits.

Moreover, the 1930s Great Depression engulfed rural Texas, persuading Erath County farmers to implement conservation measures heretofore untried and, more importantly, to embrace crop diversification. While wheat and oats never became major regional crops, even before the Depression years, Erath County small grains production leapt in 1870 from 78,109 bushels to 2,548,000 in 1900. As cotton production declined, other sectors of the economy like poultry, peanuts, and fruit orchards grew. The nursery business became an important component of Stephenville's rural economy. The dairy industry, however, owned the future.

During the early 1930s, many county farmers abandoned row crops for dairying. By 1900, Erath County was already home for a number of well-regarded registered Jersey herds. As the century progressed—particularly by the 1970s—Holstein herds became the county's principal dairy cow. The 1913 establishment of the Stephenville Creamery gave a welcome boost to dairy farmers, as did the 1934 arrival of Triangle Produce Company, which purchased whole milk and shipped it to nearby Comanche County to be turned into cheese. Three years later, construction of a milk -processing plant in Stephenville further fueled dairy interests, giving farmers an even closer place to convert surplus milk to cheese. By 1972, the county boasted 15,500 dairy cattle that produced 155 million pounds of milk, valued at $10 million. The dairy industry is so successful today that Stephenville proudly proclaims itself the "Dairy Capital of Texas."

If Stephenville and Erath County remain inherently rural, the post–World War II era has witnessed modest manufacturing and industrial growth. Today St. Gobain Abrasives and FMC Technologies are major employers in the city. Schreiber Foods, affectionately known by locals as "the Cheese Plant," is another important business. In retail, H-E-B Grocers employs 120 people. Wal-Mart Supercenter provides jobs for 385 people and offers residents of Erath County shopping options that keep its parking lot full on weekends. If the Stephen brothers, proprietors of Stephenville's first general store, were alive today, they would marvel at the range of products available along Wal-Mart's aisles. They would also be astonished at the "horseless carriages" ensconced in Wal-Mart's modern version of the hitching post. Many of those cars were purchased at Stephenville's two successful, longtime automobile dealerships, Bruner Motors and Texstar Ford.

Another important Stephenville business component is the medical industry. Stephenville has come a long way from 1860, when Dr. William W. McNeill—son-in-law of John M. Stephen and sixth-wealthiest resident in Erath County—was Stephenville's only physician and one of only four Erath County doctors. From Dr. J. C. Terrell's 1926 establishment of Stephenville's first hospital to the operation of today's Harris Methodist Hospital and Stephenville Medical and Surgical Clinic, quality health care for residents of Stephenville and surrounding areas has been beneficent.

City and county government employs 245 people. Nancy Hunter is Stephenville's second two-term female mayor; the first was Lavina Lohrmann, who was also the first SISD female board member. The mayoral office demonstrates the degree that gender roles have shifted since 1860. The most common occupation of residents of Erath County then was not farmer, stock raiser, or planter, but house keeper, the vocation of 375 Erath County women. Over 150 years, not only have local political roles become open to women, but also during the late 20th and early 21st centuries, Stephenville women have served as top administrators at all levels of Erath County government, as chamber of commerce president, as managing editor of the local Stephenville Empire-Tribune, and as public school administrators.

Education is today's largest Stephenville employer. Tarleton State University's payroll provides for 900 people. The Stephenville Independent School District employs another 450. This emphasis starkly contrasts to the education in the years after Stephenville's 1855 establishment. As in most frontier communities, schooling was necessarily minimal. In 1860, Erath County boasted a meager dozen teachers for 46 students. Nevertheless, several educational pioneers laid the foundation for what today is the centerpiece of both community employment and culture.

The most conspicuous example is John Tarleton, a New England–born Erath County merchant-rancher whose $85,000 bequest revived the defunct Stephenville College, which was chartered in 1893 and renamed John Tarleton College in 1899. An orphan before the age of 10, Tarleton was denied the opportunity for education. He parleyed his considerable assets into help for unfortunate others. Through its various 20th-century evolutions, the institution has become today's Tarleton State University, which has been agriculturally oriented throughout its history. Today it is the most important institution of higher learning for Erath and bordering counties.

Public education in Stephenville has likewise improved since its inception. By the early 1860s, primitive log cabin schoolhouses appeared, starting first at Gilbreath, 3 miles east of town. A recognizable public school system began soon after the Civil War, with the 1867 establishment of 13 county school districts. By 1917, that number had grown to 132. In 1937, Erath County had 124 teachers and 3,057 students in its rural schools. In Stephenville, 33 of those teachers taught 1,008 students.

The late 20th and early 21st centuries transformed Stephenville public education. A number of schools in SISD have earned exemplary status. In both academics and athletics, students have brought countless individual and team state titles to the "City of Champions," where, as from earliest days, locals love a winner. In pioneer times, Stephenville's citizens measured the mettle of the community by performances in spelling bees, debate competitions, local horse races, and even chicken fights. Such diversions were welcome distractions from mundane, workday challenges of frontier life. While the form of competition has changed, the drive to win and the desire to succeed remains.

The 21st century's daily challenges differ from those in decades past, but Stephenville's residents are no less enthused about the accomplishments and achievements, be it in the classroom, on the field of play, or on the stage for musical or theatrical performances. Success in the rodeo arena has led locals to style the city as the "Cowboy Capital of the World." As the challenges of demographic changes and new diversities appear on Erath County's horizon, Stephenville's businesses, local government, and educational institutions are ready and able to preserve the city's championship tradition in a rapidly evolving community and world.

One

SETTLERS AND ANGLO-CELTIC CIVILIZATION

If Stephen F. Austin brought the "Old Three Hundred" to colonize Mexican Texas, it seems equally true that Erath and Stephen brought an "Old Thirty" to found both Stephenville and Erath County. Local legend suggests that this 1855 nucleus of 30 pioneers transformed a Caddo Indian village, situated along the Bosque River, into the settlement of Stephenville.

Few images of the original founding settlers have survived, but visual evidence of institutions they established and infrastructure they laid abounds. No greater symbol of respect for law, and order, and sanctity of private property can be found than the county courthouse. In 1857, settlers erected Stephenville's first courthouse, a building made of rawhide lumber in Block 3, located on the city square's east side. At least part of that edifice, along with all county records, burned in 1866, and the building was eventually replaced in 1876 by Stephenville's first stone courthouse. This two-story building served until 1891, when fire again destroyed the edifice. Subsequently, the Erath County Commissioners Court accepted the design of San Antonio architect J. Riely Gordon for the building sitting atop the square today.

Reliable postal service appeared soon after Stephenville's founding, ensuring communication between the residents of this new Texas outpost and the outside world. Not long after John M. Stephen assumed his 1857 duties as Stephenville's first postmaster, post offices proliferated in fledgling hinterland communities. By 1879, post offices existed in Armstrong, Bluff Dale, Duffau, Dublin, Erath, Harpers Hill, Morgan Mill, Paluxy, Rock Falls, Rocky, Shiloh, and Squaw Creek.

Another trait of Southern civilization borne by original settlers was passionate religious faith. The Stephen and McNeill families quickly organized a proper Methodist Church. The Baptists however, led by "Choctaw Bill" Robinson, soon dominated numerically. Presbyterians became a religious force as well. From that day until this, these denominations, and subsequently many others, have exerted one of the strongest influences shaping the quality and character of Stephenville society and culture.

Kay Walton's interpretation depicts the arrival of Erath and Stephen with their scouting party along the banks of the Bosque River. In the background, Thomas Arendell and Dr. W. W. McNeill inspect the riverbank. Friendly Anadarko chief Jose Maria assists, while a Comanche scout menacingly lurks in the foliage at the left. Titled *New Eden*, the painting depicts authentic 1850s flora. (Scott and Jenny Allen.)

In his late teens, George B. Erath (1813–1891) migrated from Vienna, Austria, to New Orleans, Cincinnati, and eventually Mexican Texas. There, as a private, he fought at San Jacinto in Company C of Col. Edward Burleson's First Regiment, Texas Volunteers. Erath surveyed numerous Central Texas locations, including the site of Stephenville.

Although no pictures of John M. Stephen have survived, his grave marker still stands in the Stephen family plot in Stephenville's West End Cemetery. (Above, Debbie Cashell; at right, Maddi Cashell.)

JOHN M.
STEPHEN
BORN DEC
29 1814
DIED MAR
31 1862

Original settler William Franklin Stephen is pictured above (first row, second from left) with his family. He settled along Resley's Creek on the Sion Blythe Survey, near where the city of Dublin developed in southwestern Erath County. Dr. William W. McNeill (at left) also was among the first to settle Stephenville. On December 17, 1854, McNeill married John M. Stephen's daughter, Mary Arbilla, not long before pioneers completed Stephenville's survey. In 1862, McNeill became administrator of his deceased father-in-law's sizable estate. Stephenville's trouble with the Native Americans dated from Arch McNeill's killing of a drunken Anadarko, Red Jack, after which Jose Maria and his tribesmen ceased to act as a buffer between the new arrivals and hostile Comanche.

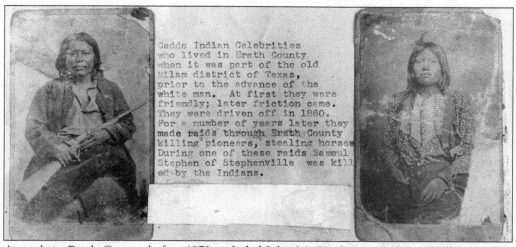

Caddo Indian Celebrities who lived in Erath County when it was part of the old Milam district of Texas, prior to the advance of the white man. At first they were friendly; later friction came. They were driven off in 1860. For a number of years later they made raids through Erath County killing pioneers, stealing horses During one of these raids Sameul Stephen of Stephenville was killed by the Indians.

Arrivals in Erath County before 1870 included John M. Stephen's son James Miller Stephen (1846–1920), located in the first row and second from left (below). The Mefford, Arnold, and Roberts families (all whose placement is conjectural) had family members present for the Fourth of July completion of Stephenville's survey. When settlers, led by Erath, Stephen, and Neill McLennan, arrived in 1855, a Caddo settlement likely stood along the river's bank. Relations between settlers and Native Americans were peaceful, until the self-appointed Erath County Rangers attacked a friendly Caddo-Anadarko encampment at Young County's Golconda on December 27, 1858. This "Lower Brazos Reserve Massacre" (as described by Sherri Knight in *Vigilantes to Verdicts*) resulted in the deaths of seven Indians and Samuel Stephen (John's son, a victim of "friendly fire"). Subsequently, Comanche tribesmen troubled Stephenville's fledgling settlement, stealing cattle and horses and killing some along the edge of settlement.

Pioneers -- all Ca....
Stephenville before 1870

PIONEERS OF STE...
1. Mr. Kelly
2. James Stephens
3. Mr. Mefford
4. Mr. Arnold
5. L. F. Evans
6. George Lydia
7. L. F. Roberts
8. Jimmy Roberts
9. Cash Tolliver

15

Uncle Ike Gasy — Aunt Sarah
(Slaves)

Aunt Nancy
Kennedy — (A Slave)

Although records about Erath County's early African American population are rare, its members were among the county's earliest residents. John M. Stephen left some slaves along a Bosque post oak grove after his 1854 reconnaissance mission. They traded beeves with local Native Americans for deerskins, bear meat, and honey. Slave descendants like Ike Gasy and Sarah (above) and Nancy Kennedy (at left), lived largely in a small, isolated community on the town's northeast side. During Reconstruction, the local freedmen's position deteriorated, a result of the rise of sharecropping combined with an influx of skilled white postwar refugees. These changes greatly reduced the demand for skilled laborers who were also African American.

Thomas Arendell was among Stephenville's earliest settlers. He erected the first log house that became the standard form of city construction. Although no image of Arendell's house survives, many photographs of the variety of 19th-century Erath County log cabins exist. Above is a two-story structure on the Dutchman branch of Resley's Creek, built in the 1850s by original settler William Franklin Stephen. The Skipper log cabin below—home for Tennessee migrant William Skipper (1822–1892)—is yet another early architectural form, albeit more primitive than the structure pictured above, of houses typically built in early Stephenville and Erath County.

William Skipper (at left) moved to Erath County in 1860. Skipper farmed and raised livestock. His interest in politics led to service as Erath County's fifth sheriff (1864–1865), a position he relinquished after the Civil War when he refused to take the Ironclad Oath, a declaration that he had never voluntarily aided the Confederacy. Sheriffs like Skipper, before and after, eventually stabilized conditions on the fringe of settlement. Some historians of the American frontier suggest that the first three structures erected by advancing Anglo-Celtic civilization were a jail, a courthouse, and a church. Each met unique needs for fledgling communities. All three building types appeared early after Stephenville's establishment. Below is Stephenville's imposing jail that was built after approval in 1905 of a $75,000 bond ballot. (At left, Marshall Sherrod; below, Wayne Sherrod.)

Above, at the 20th anniversary of the Civil War's end, the Stephenville brass band, formed in the mid-1880s, stands in cadet gray uniforms in front of Erath County's first stone courthouse. Sheriff John Gilbreath stands in the doorway. Below, Kay Walton's interpretation of the scene captures the gathering's movement and excitement. J. D. Parnell and J. J. Porter completed the courthouse's first story by March 1876. In November, the firm of Walker and White received a contract to complete the building. Two 1891 fires on the courthouse square's west and south sides—one in January and the other in the spring—inspired a petition prompting Erath County Commissioners to approve $80,000 for construction of a new county courthouse. (Below, Scott and Jenny Allen.)

The new courthouse was largely Stephenville's rejoinder to Dublin's aggressive attempt to relocate the county seat southeast. In this era marked by the exuberant spirit of Progressivism, a booming Texas economy, and a love for grand public buildings, the 1881 Texas Legislature issued financial bonds for just such construction. Stephenville prevailed. On June 24, 1891, Erath County awarded their commission to San Antonio architects, 27-year-old J. Riely Gordon and D. E. Laub. Below, workers build the 1892 courthouse on a foundation made of stone from the previous courthouse. (At left, James Riely Gordon Collection, the Alexander Architectural Archive, the University of Texas Libraries, the University of Texas at Austin [JRGC]; below, Wayne Sherrod.)

Riely Gordon (1863–1937) had an innovative expertise and produced no less than 15 Texas courthouses. His Stephenville composition was a magnificent Victorian Romanesque Revival structure made from native white limestone and red Pecos sandstone. Gordon's courthouse tower allowed for good natural ventilation and airflow through the entire building. During its lifespan, the 1892 courthouse witnessed a variety of transportation modes. Above, late-19th-century carriages and wagons transport visitors to the city square. Henry Ford's early-20th-century democratization of the automobile gave Erath County residents a new means of travel. Thereafter, scenes like the one below, with automobiles encircling the courthouse, became increasingly typical. (Below, Marilyn Giesecke Ewers.)

At left, Lillie Gibson, Dr. C. Richard King, and Nancy Allen appear, from left to right, behind the Erath County Courthouse historical marker, which was dedicated on November 11, 1997. The ceremony—part of a Veterans Day memorial program hosted by the American Legion Turnbow Higgs Post 240—included marker placement and dedication on the southeast corner of the courthouse square. Although Stephenville's early years abound with tales of vigilante justice and law enforcement by the "mob," law and order eventually assumed a more traditional form. Justices of the peace like post–Civil War, northwest Louisiana migrant to Erath County, Terrell Bryan, hastened the arrival of the rule of law. (At left, Nancy Allen; below, Diana Quinn.)

In her recent volume, *Vigilantes to Verdicts*, local author Sherri Knight details Erath County's evolution from night riders and "Judge Lynch" to the hanging of Tom Wright, the lawful outcome of a court verdict rooted in due process. The 29th Judicial District Court found Wright guilty for the very public murder of Dublin sheriff John Adams. Wright's November 10, 1899, hanging brought hundreds of spectators to Stephenville. Since law prohibited public executions, Stephenville sheriff Tutt Hume constructed an enclosed, two-story gallows with a small window through which Wright addressed onlookers immediately before his execution. Among Wright's final words was an admonition to youth to "let liquor alone."

Stephenville

Stephenville, Erath County

INTO ETERNITY.

The Slayer of John Adams at Dublin in 1897 Pays the Penalty of the Broken Law.

TOM WRIGHT HANGED TODAY.

The History of the Crime and the Trial--Every Effort Possible Made by Friends to Save his Life by Legal Means.

WRIGHT'S DYING STATEMENT.

He Absolves Frank Leslie from Complicity in the Murder of Adams---He has Made Peace with his God and Forgives Everyone and Asks to be Forgiven.

IN BRIEF.

Tom Wright shot down Constable John Adams on Black Jack

old haunts and associates he was naturally watched from the start, and being caught in violation of

Tales of mischief and lawbreaking are colorful, but early Erath County's majority seemed comprised of stolid, law-abiding churchgoers. Their day-to-day concerns focused on creating infrastructure—transportation and communication networks tying the county's outlying areas to Stephenville. Postal service developed in Skipper's Gap and Clairette where, significantly, two of the earliest postmasters were rather postmistresses, Amanda Skipper (above, second from left) and Alwilda Johnson (at left). Johnson received mail dropped into her home through a mail slot on her outside wall. When she stepped down in 1903, letters cost 2¢ to mail. Skipper and her siblings Henry, Welty, and Edna appear at their 1905 home where the post office was housed. Johnson and Skipper anticipated two modern Stephenville characteristics, reliable mail service and gender equity. In recent decades, countless women have held top administrative positions in government, education, and media. (Above, Marshall Sherrod; at left, Glenda Stone)

No 19th-century Christian denominations adapted better than the Methodists and Baptists to religious needs of migrants on the Southern frontier. Predictably, these two denominations dominated early in Erath County. Ministers William Harvey Davis (left) and W. M. Green (right) appear above at an August 1911 mass baptism in Gilmore Creek, near Altman, following a W. M. Green association tent meeting. Meanwhile, Methodist Christianity was the preference of many of Stephenville's best-known founders. As late as the 1870s, Stephenville Methodists still met in the two-story Masonic Lodge, located northwest of the square at Mason and Belknap Streets, sharing the facility week-by-week with the Baptists and Presbyterians. Although it took a while, by 1910, Methodist brethren enjoyed the comforts of the structure shown below.

In 1917, just two blocks west of the town square, an attractive domed structure with giant Corinthian columns and stained glass windows became the largest Methodist house of worship for Stephenville residents. This same facility, shown above, remains home for Stephenville's largest Methodist community today. In 1988, the historical marker at left commemorated the establishment of the Methodist church serving the Stephenville community from 1855 to the present. (Left, Debbie Cashell.)

Prior to Reconstruction, Erath County Baptists knew the three main Baptists preachers as "The Three R's," "Choctaw Bill" Robinson, "Comanche Rube" Ross, and Isaac Reed (the grandson of the 1830s and 1840s East Texas Baptist minister with the same name). In absence of more traditional church buildings, these men often assembled their congregations for brush arbor meetings and convocations in vacant log cabins. Eventually, fine buildings like Stephenville's early-20th-century First Baptist Church replaced outdoor gatherings. More recently, the First Baptist Church complex below is one of Stephenville's largest churches in facilities and worshippers. (Above, CTHI:DSLC; below, Debbie Cashell.)

Other denominations developing large memberships in the late 19th century were the Presbyterian Church (at left), Christian Church, and the Church of Christ (above about 1950). Today the Presbyterian church shown here stands on the grounds of the Stephenville Historical Museum and is the venue for weddings, musicals (including an annual St. Valentine's Day event), book launchings such as Sherri's Knight's *Tom P's Fiddle*, fund-raisers, tours, and meetings for various local groups and organizations. The movie *An Acrid Yarn* was even filmed there.

Two

ALL AROUND THE SQUARE

While the Erath County Courthouse is the architectural heart and soul of Stephenville, this creation of celebrated courthouse architect J. Riely Gordon has two "first cousins" positioned on the courthouse's southwestern and northwestern flanks. The striking Gordon structures that grace the downtown landscape are First National Bank and Crow's Opera House. Both are recipients of esteemed Texas historical landmark plaques (1994 and 1977, respectively).

Today neither of these Gordon buildings performs the function for which they were originally designed, yet both remain coveted and recognizable local landmarks. A pictorial tour around the square tells much of Stephenville's story from its 1855 origins to recent times. Many original buildings encircling the courthouse remain with only minor modifications. The evolution of purpose and proprietors reveals much about how the needs, interests, and activities of Stephenville's citizens have changed with the times.

Chapter two provides a visual tour "all around the square," starting with Gordon's First National Bank, which adorns the corner of Belknap and East College Streets. Moving clockwise, the following imagery rehearses the tale of a town in transition. It captures the story of Stephenville when Cage and Crow Bank, Robertson and Minter, Farmers National Bank, Higginbotham Company, and other highly patronized establishments, located only a few blocks away, were popular and familiar places. There, Erath County's residents congregated to shop, to do business, to deposit and withdraw their money, and to nourish friendships with those they met around the square.

As time passed and the needs and interests of Stephenville's citizenry have changed, so have some of the memorable landmarks that today's younger generation never knew. The courthouse is encircled by a blend of buildings, old and new. Counting the one for the courthouse, four historical markers document the rich and venerable story of how Stephenville blossomed into the developed, lively city it is today.

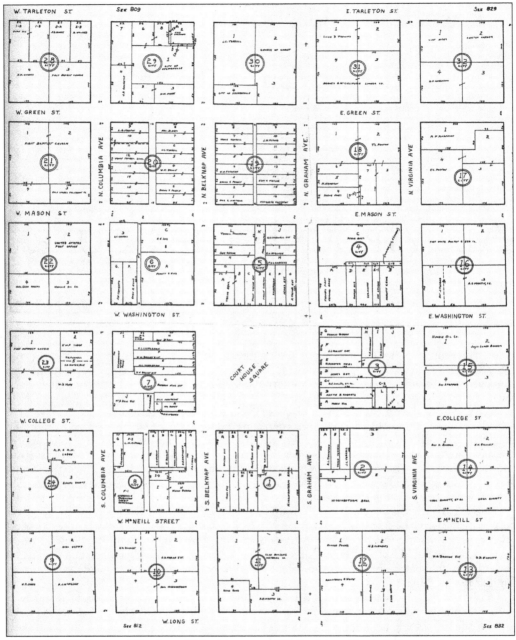

Above is a 1956 map of Stephenville's city square. While this grid postdates creation of the city by more than a century, the layout of streets surrounding the public square remains as it was when Erath and his fellow surveyors completed their task on July 4, 1855. This chapter is a tour of the square and its surrounding area, starting at the southeast corner where Belknap and College Streets intersect. (Erath County clerk of court.)

Of all the buildings around the square, perhaps First National Bank (above)—J. Riely Gordon's first Stephenville masterpiece—deserves status as the crown jewel structure adjacent to the courthouse. Constructed in 1889 to house Stephenville's first bank, it combines Romanesque Revival architecture with a Queen Anne–style tower. Thanks to the labors of local preservationists, its facade remains much as it originally was. The introduction of banking to Stephenville marks the ultimate local evolution of the mid-19th-century barter economy into a modern cash-based system. A frontal view of the First National Bank (facing southeast) appears below. (Above, CTHI: Baxley Collection [BC]; below, Nancy Allen.)

Above, architect J. Riely Gordon works in his San Antonio office. At age 18, Gordon apprenticed in the San Antonio office of architect W. K. Dobson. In 1883, Gordon joined the staff of Supervising Architect of the U.S. Treasury in Washington, D.C. He returned to San Antonio in 1885 and, in 1886, founded the Texas State Association of Architects. In 1887, Gordon opened his own office. In 1902, Gordon moved his practice to New York City, where he was a 13-term president of the New York Society of Architects. Below, the interior of First National Bank appears with several bank clerks at their stations about 1900. (Above, JRGC; below, Nancy Allen.)

A December 7, 1897, fire in Perry's (adjacent to First National Bank) burned half the city block. First National appears above right after its restoration. Previously, the bank was not bedecked by the distinctive pointed tower that sits atop the building today. To the north of First National Bank, R. E. Cox Dry Goods store (below) eventually did business in the center of the block. This dry goods store witnessed the transition from the horse-and-buggy age to the age of the automobile. (Above, Nancy Allen.)

The image above shows a bustling crowd of people and cars patronizing a sale at Cox's. To the immediate north is Ellis and Creswell Drugstore. Yet further up the bock, a new corner drugstore (below) was completed with Thurber brick in 1899. It had many incarnations, being owned successively by the Schnabel, White, Swan Richardson, D'Arcy, Riddick, and Baker families, and finally Eckerd Drug Company. Until 1994, these drugstores traded on the square's northwest corner during the 20th century. Their success was commemorated in 2009 by the historical marker now adorning the building's north side. (Below, CTHI:BC.)

Immediately across Washington Street from the drugstore was Carlton Brothers (above), built in 1901. The structure burned in 1914. This lot is today's site of Stephenville's Cowboy Walk of Fame. Crow's Opera House (below), another Gordon masterpiece, stands immediately east across Belknap Street. This imposing native limestone Romanesque structure was originally Erath County National Bank, but soon became the Cage and Crow Bank building. The 1893 death of bank president Dr. M. S. Crow led to voluntary liquidation of the bank. Three years before her husband's decease, Mollie Jane Crow turned the building's second floor into a thriving cultural facility, seating some 400 people and providing a venue for theater productions, dances, and other social fetes. (Above, Wayne Sherrod; below Nancy Allen.)

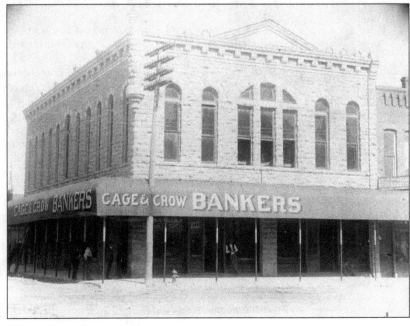

1916

Moving to the northeast corner, where Graham and Washington Streets intersect, Baxter and Francis Furniture (formerly the Neblett Building and today's site of Bank of America) is shown above in 1916. While not directly on the square, another of Stephenville's distinctive landmarks, Oxford House, sits on Graham Street's east side, five blocks north of the courthouse. The historical marker, erected in 1994, highlights the structure's majestically done late Queen Anne architectural style as well as its "cypress wraparound porch, second-level balcony, ornately detailed woodwork, character-defining cupola, and a copper eagle weather vane" (as described on the marker). Built between 1898 and 1899, this Victorian house was home for Judge W. J. Oxford (1861–1943). For a time after his wife's death, Oxford rented the house to the lawyers shown at left. (Above, Wayne Sherrod.)

Numerous businesses prospered south down Graham Street, as shown below along the eastern block of the square. Above, the Oxford Building (a law and abstract office), Robertson and Minter, and B. F. Compton once conducted business in the middle of the block. The Oxford Building featured transoms and detailed tinwork at the top of building. To the far right was B. F. Compton's Tin Shop. Local tradition suggests Compton made the tinwork on the Oxford Building. Businesses came and went on the square's east side. R. E. Cox Drugs (below, right) proved a popular place for customers. (Above, Nancy Allen.)

East Side Public Square, Stephenville, Texas

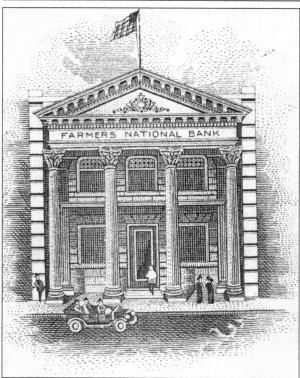

Following its 1907 opening, Cox's drugstore (above) served customers with style. In the year before, Farmers National Bank was founded but operated on the square's north side. Under leadership of the Frey family, in 1909, Farmers National moved into its newly constructed facility (at left), built on the square's east side, occupying the space where Robertson and Minter grocers previously operated. The new bank facade was made of crushed granite fixed with cement to make the blocks on the building's front. It featured four attractive Corinthian columns. Its ornamental details included corbelled granite work, pronounced keystones, and elaborate granite scrollwork in panels surmounting name and date. The upper shelf and windows have since been removed. The outside of the building is stuccoed to cover the scars. (At left, Nancy Allen.)

The image above shows Thurber brick stacked on the square's southeast side sometime after 1929. Although brick streets encircling the square have long since been covered with asphalt, some Stephenville streets remain made of the high-quality bricks produced in Thurber, which is located 26 miles northwest of town. A historical marker erected in 1978 celebrates those thoroughfares, not far from the square, on Vanderbilt Street. Meanwhile, also just beyond the square, in around 1900, many blacksmith shops were available. One of the first was H. L. Snapp's Blacksmith and Wood Shop (below), which was operated by Snapp (right) and Jesse M. Parnell (left) and situated on the northwest corner of College and Virginia Streets in Lot 1, Block 14. (Above, J. D. Walker.)

Above, customers flock to Higginbotham Company, taking advantage of a 1909 mid-summer sale. Higginbotham's operated at the intersection of Graham and College Streets. Higginbotham's, with other businesses fronting College Street, burned in 1891. The facility, shown above, was under construction the same time the present courthouse was built. In a day prior to Erath County's enforcement of the "Local Option," when locals were given the right to vote on making Erath County wet or dry in 1902, Bill Dawson's Palace Saloon was at the west end of College Street. The horse-drawn carriages above were soon replaced by automobiles. Higginbotham's operated a Ford dealership from the back of its building along Graham Street. The 1895 photograph below shows Compton Dry Goods in the middle of the south block, facing College Street. Further to the west, a shaving parlor existed.

Three

FROM CATTLE TO COTTON

In Central Texas during the late 1840s, Jacob DeCordova worked hand in glove with George B. Erath. The latter surveyed, and the former sold newly opened Texas lands. On September 28, 1858, DeCordova addressed England's Midlands textile producers in Manchester, proclaiming Texas the next cotton planter's *el dorado*, "golden one." Cotton's potential along the Bosque River's banks did not escape notice of Erath County's earliest settlers. Nevertheless, during its first two decades, stock raising and cattle ranches dominated the economy. There were, however, men like planter James C. Drew from Carroll Parish, Louisiana. With 960 stock cattle, he was the second largest stockholder in 1860 Erath County. Drew also brought 40 of his extended family's 100 slaves to Texas. His 1860 purchase from John M. Stephen of 480 acres along the Bosque suggests that the Drews had more than cattle ranching as a long-term goal.

Drew and Stephen fit the antebellum pattern peopling America's virgin agricultural frontier lands virtually from the Jamestown Colony's founding. Fortunes were made by stouthearted pioneers willing to tap the natural resources and advantages in front of settlers moving on a south-by-southwesterly migratory trajectory. Drawn to the intersection of the 98th meridian and 32nd parallel by profit from cattle and cotton, Drew, Stephen, and a host of others pushed westward into Erath County, where they created the economically viable population center that remains today.

By the early 1870s, the county's economic focus had shifted from cattle to cotton. While Stephenville's founders no doubt expected the rise of a cotton economy, they likely would be surprised to see the following images, not of slaves harvesting the fleecy fiber along the riverbanks but of relatively poor white sharecropping families and impoverished white laborers picking cotton that infused Stephenville's economy with vitality until the economic winds of change shifted in the first decade of the 20th century. The Civil War and Lincoln's emancipation of the slaves may have changed the way Erath County's cotton crop was gathered, but not the fact that for a moment on the county's cosmic clock, cotton once again was king.

Few images better capture the transition in the Erath County economy around 1900 than the one above. With cattle in the foreground and the Ward Cotton Gin in the background, this image summarizes that moment in time when cotton production, albeit for only four decades, supplanted cattle ranching as the leading sector of Erath County's economy. Before that transitory time, men like Col. W. C. Bishop (at left), a cattleman from Clairette, aimed to make a fortune in the cattle business. The assets he brought to Erath County in 1873 made him the county's wealthiest cattle rancher and dealer. For a time, Bishop partnered with Richard Head. (At left, Glenda Stone.)

Above, cattleman William D. Ewers and drovers tend his herd in the 1880s near Chalk Mountain, before cedar trees encroached on prairie land. Many early arrivals in mid-19th-century Erath County hoped to exploit proximity to the Chisholm Trail to turn a profit through herding and selling of bovines, easily nurtured and fattened on local waist-high grasses. Among that number was William F. Stephen, owner of the "Bar S" horse and cattle brand, who made several trips up the Chisholm Trail. Warlike Comanches confuted cattlemen's aspirations. Moreover, Erath County soils proved as benign at producing cotton as pastureland. Even as late as the 1920s, Erath County farmers, like the one shown at right, were still producing the cotton crops. (Above, Fred Ewers Sr.; at right, Marshall Sherrod.)

As Eli Whitney revolutionized the Old South's economy with his 1793 invention of the cotton gin, so arrival of gins in Erath County transformed economic life in both the county and in Stephenville. Thomas Arendell, a member of the Erath and Stephen reconnaissance party to the Bosque River in the spring of 1854, identified himself as a planter by 1860. Little wonder the Arendell family established its own personal gin (above). As the 20th century progressed, gins proliferated. Below, the Johnsville gin, some 13 miles east of Stephenville, appears in the early 1920s. (Below, Marshall Sherrod.)

Gorman, Texas
About 1898

Seated on the wagon, Frank Winters of Huckabay, 11 miles north of Stephenville, had a gin as well. This picture, taken in 1898, is incorrectly labeled Gorman. Below, the Kight Clairette gin sits in ruins after a 1917 explosion. From left to right, Will Johnson, Artie Thompson, and G. H. Golightly hold the two mules, Kate and Rhody, that never moved when the blast occurred. (Above, Cindy Shipman; below, Glenda Stone.)

Any cotton planting operation depended on the men, women, and children in the fields harvesting the fruit of their labors. The smiles on some faces of those cotton pickers, pictured above, suggest satisfaction from a hard day's work. In contrast, the somber expressions in the Baxley photograph below probably paints a more realistic picture. Local old-timers still alive are quick to regale willing listeners with tales of terrible toil in the fields. More than a few of the children who picked cotton from daylight until dusk resolved early on to find some occupation that would carry them as far from the cotton fields as possible.

Some Erath County families not only harvested and weighed the cotton crops grown on their own lands, but many kinship units then moved west to help there with the harvest. The Alvin "Red" Cox family, shown in the field above, eagerly embraced opportunities to make extra spending money by picking cotton in West Texas after their Erath County harvest was securely picked, bagged, and ginned. At right, a member of the Erath community sits atop freshly picked cotton loaded on the trailer and waiting to be baled. (Both, Marshall Sherrod.)

As testified above by the cotton bales brought by mules pulling wagons to the Stephenville Cotton Yard, cotton picked and ginned yielded a rich 1902 harvest. I. N. Roberts owned this yard. He paid a paltry $19 for the entire city block on which it stood (a Baptist church is located there today). Eventually, mechanized vehicles replaced wheeled transport powered by animals. Below, J. T. Lockhart's drayman flatbed wagon, weighed down with cotton bales and field hands, illustrates this significant transition.

Even high rates of cotton production did little to benefit county farmers until Stephenville secured a cost-effective means of transporting products from farm to textile producers. Lack of rail transport through Stephenville hampered the blossoming of the county's cotton crop. Local businessmen, particularly the Frey family, organized wagon trains to Alexander, which had a railroad by 1881, guaranteeing transport of cotton and other products to market until Stephenville got its own railroad in 1889. Above, J. A. Jordan (farthest left) and merchant John A. Frey's son W. H. Frey (second from left), stand with unidentified others at the W. H. Frey Dry Goods store entryway. Below, the Stephenville Roundhouse is pictured in 1888.

The Fort Worth and Rio Grande Railroad came to Stephenville in the fall of 1889. Above, Stephenville's Frisco depot appears. Meanwhile, the establishment of a local cotton oil mill gave cotton growers additional incentive to plant. As Erath County cotton production flagged throughout the 1920s and Depression years, ultimately, the Stephenville Cotton Seed Oil Company below became the Birdsong Peanut Mill. This shifting of focus represented an even wider diversification that impacted all sectors of the Stephenville economy. (Both, Wayne Sherrod.)

Four

DIVERSIFICATION, DAIRIES, AND COMING OF AGE

Many, if not most, who founded Stephenville hoped to make their fortunes on cattle. Indeed, local topsoil and native grasses were ideal for cattle ranching. Stockmen who dealt in the cattle trade hoped to make sustained use of the southern branch of the Chisholm trail—old Alexander Road—that passed within 10 miles of Stephenville. Through raids, cattle theft, and stampeding local herds, hostile Comanches frustrated the few early attempted cattle drives. Nevertheless, cattle continued to play an important role in Stephenville's economy. While the number of cows in Erath County dramatically dropped during cotton's reign, subsequently, that number increased when cotton could no longer sustain the local economy. The kind of cattle, however, began to differ. No longer would beef cows dominate. By the 1930s, an influx of dairy cows heralded the rise of the dairy industry.

Of course, not everyone relied on milk production. At long last, new and different sectors of the economy began to develop. Some were patently agricultural, namely poultry, peanuts, and fruit. Others were more diverse. During the early 20th century, the nursery business prospered vigorously in Erath County. The first nurseries were established around the start of the 20th century. There was Crocker, located 8 miles west of Stephenville; Stitton's near Dublin; Inabnet's near Alexander; Higginbotham's at Cotton Wood; and Grissett's near Johnson Cemetery. Families like the Wolfes and Fitzgeralds, to name only two, gained great financial success establishing their operations not only locally but also across the state and well beyond. Meanwhile, modern and sophisticated medical treatment also reached Stephenville. In 1935, Dr. Vance Terrell joined the staff of the hospital that was founded in 1926 by his brother J. C. Terrell. By 1980, Stephenville Hospital admitted no less than 3,600 patients annually, served another 3,500 each year at the Stephenville Medical and Surgical Clinic, and employed 130 doctors and staff. Today's Harris Methodist Hospital employs 300 area residents, while the Stephenville Clinic has 140—which is 10 more than the entire hospital staff only a decade ago—on its payroll.

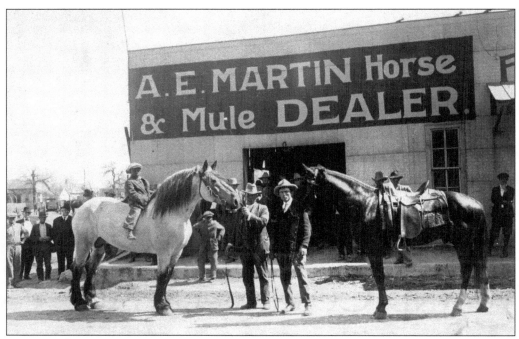

In 1915, with Europe at war, A. E. Martin Horse and Mule Dealer (above) exploited the demand for mules, making Saturdays "Mule Day." Martin was particularly interested in mules 8 to 14 hands high, eight years old or younger, and suitable for use in war. Throughout the early 20th century, mules and draft horses remained a prerequisite for farming success. Below, at the foot of Lone Mountain, from left to right, George Sherrod, his son (probably Jesse), Pete Ewers, Virge Martin, Isam Martin (driver), Lanham Martin (binder operator), and their mule team are harvesting small grains with a McCormick-Deering binder. During the 1910s, cultivation of wheat, oats, and rye supplanted the cotton culture that dominated from the 1870s through 1910. Crop diversification flourished until the 1930s, when the dairy industry established local dominance. (Below, Marshall Sherrod.)

Hay baling crews (above) were familiar sites in Erath County during the Depression years. The Wiley Thompson farm at Bunyan illustrates the importance of the county's hay crop. From left to right are (seated) John East and Bob Templeton; (standing) Bill Thompson, Harmon Grissom, and Milton Templeton. As the 20th century progressed, mechanization made the lives of farmers easier. The tractor and peanut combine at the West Cross Timbers Experiment Station, shown below, depicts how far farming methods had advanced by the mid–20th century. With the conversion of Stephenville's cottonseed oil mill into the Birdsong Peanut Mill, the peanut combine became particularly useful, highlighting a new component in the diversifying Erath County economy. (Above, Brad Thompson.)

While Erath County farmers placed emphasis on multiple new undertakings, none had the impact of the dairy industry. The 1972 construction of Moo-La the Cow (below), located on the northeast corner of the courthouse square, celebrated the late-20th-century dominance that the area's dairy farmers had established in Texas. The September 23, 1972, unveiling took place to the musical backdrop provided by dairyman Jimmie Don Pack and his country and western band. Speeches by Dr. Vance Terrell (who, in addition to his medical practice, owned and operated a local dairy) and Col. Dave Montgomery (whose support and contributions helped make Moo-La possible) focused on the significance of the dairy business to the Erath County economy. As the dairy industry waxed strong, dairy herds, in abundance, dotted the Erath County landscape. The herd above drinks water near the Bosque River. (Above, Debbie Cashell.)

The dairy herd above waits patiently by the dairy farm water trough to be milked. In 1948, longtime dairyman W. L. Payton's 25 Jersey cows (below) produced the highest percentage of butterfat of any herd in Texas. Many Stephenville youths benefited greatly from the Future Farmers of America chapter at the high school, an organization that enabled them to prepare early for future careers in the dairy or cattle-raising industries.

Although the poultry business never assumed the stature of the dairy industry, it also flourished during the mid–20th century. Stephenville's hinterland farmers took advantage of this opportunity. Below, Walter Little feeds his chickens on a farm in eastern Erath County in 1927. Around the same time, Elva Parnell Sherrod nurtures her turkey chicks on the family farm at left. She also sold her abundant supply of chicken eggs in Stephenville to Triangle Produce Company. A symbiotic, reciprocal relationship tied farmers on the county periphery to produce companies in the county seat. Companies like Triangle even came to the farms on the outer edges of the county to pick up chicks and baby turkeys. (Both, Marshall Sherrod.)

In the city itself, poultry farms, like the one above, bolstered the local economy. Stephenville's turkey market (below) was also an important Erath County industry. During the 1940s, the Santa Fe Railroad regularly shipped carloads of turkeys out of the city to eager consumers throughout the state. Stephenville's hatcheries, combined with homegrown birds provided by the hinterland, ensured a steady supply of poultry sold in the "Lone Star State."

57

The image below shows a historical 1911 convocation of American Civil War veterans on the northern Earth County Courthouse steps. If industrialization in the north accelerated rapidly after that conflict, southern states like Texas remained highly agricultural, especially in smaller urban centers like Stephenville. The next great conflict, World War I, sent scores of Erath County residents off to France. Above, one group that was preparing to serve America poses at the courthouse. The Great War stimulated American industrial development, but once again, Erath County retained its rural personae. Some Stephenville residents, however, exploited marketing opportunities ripe for the harvest. No better example exists than the Erath County nursery business.

In the first decade of the 20th century, Luther Burbank encouraged Ross Wolfe to leave California, return to his native Texas, and start a pecan nursery. Wolfe left the "Golden State." In 1918, he and wife, Mabel, came to Erath County and built one of Texas's largest nursery businesses. Wolfe opened shop on 60 acres of sandy soil, located 2 miles west of town. Headquarters was the unique rock house (above) that was made from petrified rock, serpent stones, fossils, copper ore, quartz, and even a dinosaur track taken from the Paluxy River. It was a one-of-a-kind, signature Stephenville landmark and was featured in *Ripley's Believe it or Not* strip as "The House that Time Built." Ross's son, the millionaire businessman and professional football star, Hugh Wolfe, designed the distinctive Wolfe Nursery sign. The sign below also became a nationally recognized symbol. (Above, Nancy Allen.)

Today the former Wolfe Nursery property (above) is the site of Jack in the Box, Staples, Wal-Mart, and a small shopping center. Below, Joe Fitzgerald, who attended Stephenville's McIlhaney Academy and published the *Ghost of the McDow Hole* stories, grew grapes, apples, pears, pecans, plums, peaches, and berries, but his claim to fame came primarily from the Eureka persimmon, which produced four bushels to the tree. *Farm and Ranch* magazine christened him "Persimmon Joe." Below, 1920s Fitzgerald Nursery employees congregate for a group photograph. Included in the back row are Herbert Johnson (ninth from left), Ed Dawson (third from right), Howard Johnson, (second from right) and Joe Fitzgerald (farthest right). (Below, Glenda Stone.)

WATER WORKS OF STEPHENVILLE

A readily available water supply was, of course, necessary for Erath County nurseries to prosper. Likewise, mid-19th-century settlers needed water as well. During the early years, few town water wells existed. Those that did were nowhere close to the square or residential district. Consequently, Stephenville's first utility, the water works, was a two-wheeled horse-drawn cart and barrel. From these primitive beginnings, Jim Manskar (above), a black resident affectionately known as "Uncle Jim," sold his product for 10¢ to 25¢ a bucket. As decades passed, public service advanced. At right, J. Louis Evans (left), Stephenville mayor from 1956 to 1964, is shown in more recent times, as he and an unidentified colleague prepare to christen the State Department of Health sign that approved the city water supply.

Beyond clean drinking water, another prerequisite of a happy, healthy community is adequate medical care. In 1926, Dr. J. C. Terrell (at left) established the hospital in Stephenville that continues to serve Erath County residents today. That same year, an 18-year-old Carl A. Phillips (below) took a "temporary" job at the hospital. Phillips subsequently served Dr. Terrell and the hospital until his 1993 retirement. Phillips continued to work as a hospital volunteer until his death in 2006 at age 98. Shown below with two nurses, he models a new sport coat. In 2005, Tarleton State University acknowledged Phillips's rich and remarkable community service, awarding him an honorary doctor of humane letters degree. (Below, Harris Methodist Hospital.)

December 2008

Texas Monthly

IT'S OVER!
by PAUL BURKA

The 40 Best Small-Town Cafes

Chicken-fried steak. Cherry pie. Hot coffee. And some friendly gossip.

(see page 124)

Jake and Dorothy's Cafe, in Stephenville

texasmonthly.com | $4.95

1 2>

0 74851 18450 9

THE FUGITIVE HOUSEWIFE by Skip Hollandsworth
REMEMBER THE FLORIDA RECOUNT? by Brian D. Sweany
THE PILGRIM'S PRIDE IMMIGRATION RAID by Karen Olsson

During the first few decades after settlers filled Erath County, self-sufficient farm families provided their own food with meat and grains; vegetables were a rarity until the late 19th century. In time, grocery stores appeared in town. As Stephenville neared the mid–20th century, restaurants even became an option. No example is better-known than Jake and Dorothy's Cafe, established in 1948, three blocks east of the square on Washington Street. What Jake and Dorothy Roach began six decades ago has stood the test of time. The December 2008 *Texas Monthly* magazine featured their establishment on the cover, naming the café in the cover article as one of the finest small town diners in Texas. (*Texas Monthly*.)

With or without *Texas Monthly* accolades, Jake and Dorothy's status locally remains iconic. Below, not long after the café opened its doors, Stephenville residents, along with folks driving through town, kept the establishment's parking lot full. It remains so today, as the restaurant's uniquely delicious chicken fried steak, white gravy, and waffle fries—among a host of other culinary delights, including a wide variety of exquisite homemade pies—keep café guests coming back for more. At left, a youthful Jake and Dorothy stroll happily on their way to attend one of the college football games that so often occupied the couple's leisure time. (Both, Kerry Roach.)

Five

CAPITAL CLAIMS

There is an inherent logic in Stephenville's double claim to be both the "Dairy Capital of Texas" and the "Cowboy Capital of the World." From earliest times, Stephenville and Erath County were conceived as a center for stock farming. The rapid mid-19th-century development of cattle ranching suggested that dairy farming had every chance of success. Moreover, today's popular sport of rodeo has its origins in cattle herding and equestrian skills required for cowboys to succeed.

Stephenville's milk production increased during the Depression years. By 1972, county dairy production generated $10 million in sales. There is little wonder that the same year Moo-La the Cow appeared on the northeast side of the square. The brainchild of Joyce and Tom Whitis, this life-size fiberglass Holstein milk cow proclaims Erath the "No. 1 Dairy County in Texas." Joyce conceived the cow's name as the ideal moniker to symbolize the phenomenal growth and contribution of Erath's dairy industry to the local economy. From the birth of Moo-La on September 23, 1972, through 2010, the value of the county's dairy production has grown to $552 million, and Erath remains the number one milk-producing county in Texas.

West of Moo-la's perch, at the intersection of Washington and Belknap Streets, is the Cowboy Capital Walk of Fame. This attractive gazebo celebrates achievements of Stephenville cowboys and cowgirls, those making an indelible mark on rodeo and Erath County's Western heritage. Since November 14, 1998, the Walk of Fame, which encircles the entire city block, has bestowed honor on Stephenville's rodeo heroes who have achieved not only local but national and worldwide successes. Among its first class of inductees was Ty Murray, "King of the Cowboys," who has gathered multiple world rodeo titles and, more recently, established himself as a ballroom dancer during season eight (2009) of *Dancing with the Stars*. A host of other worthies—some whose pictures appear in this chapter—joined Murray between 1998 and the present, including the Tarleton State University's National Intercollegiate Rodeo men's team champion of 1967 and their women's team champions of 1969, 1970, and 1971.

The recent shot of Moo-La above commemorates the claim, made by Erath County for more than 30 years, that Erath is the number one dairy county in the Lone Star State. Meanwhile, one block due east of Moo-La is the Cowboy Capital Walk of Fame, an attractive gazebo, with a marquee, that honors the achievements of Stephenville's rodeo heroes. The walk itself is on the sidewalk inside Washington, Belknap, Mason, and Columbia Streets. The plaques for each respective inductee are a kind of Texas cowboy small town answer to the celebrated forecourt of 6925 Hollywood Boulevard's Grauman's Chinese Theater. (Both, Debbie Cashell.)

W. L. Payton began selling milk to a Stephenville grocer in 1932. His Payton Jersey Farm served Erath County for four decades. In the late 1930s, Payton (above, center) and two workers prepare to milk his Jersey herd. Below, he proudly displays the bottled product that his dairy delivered to Stephenville and Erath County homes from the 1930s until 1968. At the 1948 annual meeting of the Texas Jersey Cattle Club in Abilene, Payton received a certificate designating his Jersey herd as "The Best in Texas." Payton's cow, Design Fern June, produced 14,421 pounds of milk and 669 pounds of butterfat over a one-year span. For her trouble, she received a certificate christening her the champion 1948 Jersey cow for Texas in her class and for her age. (Both, Donna Whitefield.)

Tarleton State University has always provided a cutting-edge agricultural education for students who have furthered their higher learning in Stephenville. On February 27, 2009, TSU broke ground on a new and environmentally friendly Southwest Regional Dairy Center (above), an acknowledgement of the importance not only of the dairy industry in Texas but also of the significance of the dairy business in both Stephenville and Erath County. A June 27, 2010, *Empire-Tribune* article observed that the center "was designed as a model dairy and will serve as 'the' dairy of research and learning for The Texas A&M University System." Today's Erath County dairy cow of choice—the Holstein—is found on the 697.44-acre TSU College Farm. At left, part of the Tarleton herd grazes in a fog-covered pasture. (Above, author; at left, Barry Lambert.)

Abundant Erath County dairy production makes Stephenville a logical location for the cheese plant that is owned by Schreiber Foods. As the banner on the security fence outside its main building indicates, Schreiber has been supportive not only of the local diary industry but also of the Stephenville Independent School District. Meanwhile, Schreiber gainfully employs 120 members of the Erath County community. Visitors to Stephenville encounter evidence of the influence of cattle and cowboys before even entering the town's city limits. Those driving north up Highway 377 are greeted by signage highlighting those things valued in the community. The welcome sign below salutes not only education in the local community but also the Cowboy Capital Walk of Fame. (Both photographs by author.)

In an interesting way, the above Erath County ranch scene around 1900—a cowboy standing behind his roping conquest with his fellows posing in the background— anticipates the day when Stephenville's mid-20th- and 21st-century cowboy community would demonstrate their skills in the larger, highly competitive rodeo arena. At left, moving north down Belknap Street, one sees 10 of the plaques that encircle the city block that constitutes the Stephenville Cowboy Walk of Fame. (Above, Fred Ewers Sr.; at left, Debbie Cashell.)

At right, Jim Sharp, a world-champion bull rider in 1988 and 1990, rides Sammy Andrew's "Mighty Whitey" at the 1992 Professional Rodeo Cowboys Association National Finals Rodeo in Las Vegas, Nevada. Six years later, Sharp was part of the first group of individuals inducted into the Stephenville Cowboy Walk of Fame. Below, inaugural Walk of Fame inductees were, from left to right, (first row) Jim Sharp, Ty Murray, Tuff Hedeman, Harry Tompkins, and Kay Floyd; (second row) Carolyn Colburn Holden accepting for father, Everett Colburn; George Brown accepting for himself and wife, Beulah; G. K. and Nita Brooks Lewallen; Kenneth and Betty Lesley and Bobby Foster accepting for Sherwood Foster (who also established the Stephenville Foster's Home); and Paula Wood. Kobie Wood, also inducted, is not pictured. (Both, dudleydoright.com and Joyce Whitis.)

Above, the four-time Super Bowl–winning San Francisco 49er quarterback, Joe Montana, sits astride horse Flashin' Some Cash. Montana, a friend of Kobie Wood, chose Stephenville's Lone Star Over Texas Expo Center for his June 9, 1996, inaugural ride in cutting horse competition at the Area 9 West Central Texas, North Texas, and Red River Cutting Horse Association event. Below, Whit Keeney, inducted into Stephenville's Cowboy Hall of Fame in 1999, attends a Veterans of Foreign Wars event. Texas House Resolution 985 honored the 92-year-old Keeney, who, during his lengthy rodeo career, won 37 trophy saddles, 8 consecutive all-around championships at the National Old Timers Rodeo, and, in his early years, enjoyed the distinction at the Texas Cowboy Reunion of roping with celebrated Oklahoma cowboy, folksy humorist, actor, syndicated newspaper columnist, and social commentator Will Rogers (1879–1935). (Above, *Empire-Tribune*.)

Six

RECREATIONS AND DIVERSIONS

Literature on early Erath County speaks with a united voice. Life in the 1850s on the developing frontier was hard. Even if pioneer families had excess leisure time—most did not—their spartan existence and a general absence of high culture threw early settlers on their own resources for entertainment. Children and adults alike were essentially reliant on ingenuity and creativity.

Even well into the 20th century, the record suggests that recreation in Stephenville's hinterland was often focused on simple pleasures like hunting, fishing, or playing cards, marbles, mumbley-peg, or jacks. As living standards progressively improved, new options became part of an expanding recreational repertoire, including carriage or wagon outings (and later car rides) through the countryside to popular nearby tourist sites, and even country basketball and baseball leagues. High-quality cultural diversions became increasingly common for those with access to Stephenville.

Crow's Opera House on the northwest corner of the city square probably offered the finest cultural smorgasbord. It opened in 1890 and became the venue for plays presented by both traveling stock companies and local talent, vaudeville shows, commencement exercises, annual operettas, gala dances, concerts, benefits, public readings and recitations, piano recitals, flower shows, baby shows, style shows, and even fiddling contests. In 1910, the opera house hosted the showing of Stephenville's first moving picture shows.

In 1903, the Twentieth Century Club established the Stephenville Public Library, which, in 1924, was moved from various private homes to a newly constructed building on Green and Erath Streets, a place where the log cabin of George Erath had once stood when he surveyed the city square. The Depression-era construction of the city's "Rec Hall" gave Stephenville youth enjoyable athletic options, which were lacking in the community prior to the difficult 1930s. Ray's Ornamental Gardens was a favorite tourist roadside attraction during the 1940s and 1950s. Other innovative recreational activities included barbecues hosted by well-to-do community members and annual Fourth of July festivities that included sporting events, an infinite variety of delectable delights available from visiting vendors, fireworks displays, and sometimes even armadillo races.

For 19th-century Erath County residents, equestrian skills served multiple practical purposes, including wrangling cattle, transportation to and from town, and even flight from hostile Comanche tribesmen. In July 1865, rancher Edward Cox lost his life riding after Comanches who had stolen his cattle. As descendants of the pioneers moved into the 20th century, many could finally afford to view horseback riding as a family recreation. At left, in the late 1920s, Alvin "Red" Cox, Edward's grandson, treats his nephew and niece Jack and Cloye Little to a ride on the family horse. Below, members of the Cox clan, heavily armed and with their hounds, display the stretched and dried pelts that brought them discretionary income of $45.35, which is about $568 in today's economy. Just 50 years prior, hunting skills were often requisite for furnishing the family with ample food. (Both, Marshall Sherrod.)

Cabins along the Paluxy River in adjacent Somervell County were popular tourist resorts for the well to do from urban centers larger than Stephenville. As depicted in the photograph above, Erath County plain folk like the Cox, Parnell, and Sherrod families were still able to camp along the river's banks and enjoy nature's handiwork in the first decade of the 20th century (today the site of Big Rocks Park). Means of transportation changed by the 1920s. In 1907, W. H. Crouse purchased the first car—a red Ford—bought in Stephenville. Soon, mass production enabled even rural families like George Sherrod's to afford automobiles. Pictured below, the Sherrods pose in front of their new 1924–1925 black, four-door, Model T Ford sedan, which was purchased at Stephenville's Reid Sales Ford dealership, located one block off the square and across from the Long Hotel. (Both, Marshall Sherrod.)

Be it horse races or chicken fights, from Stephenville's creation, sports have always been a welcome diversion. By the early 20th century, basketball and baseball became popular pastimes in city and country, alike. Above, four members of the Johnsville boys basketball team pose in uniform. Davis brothers "Short" and Jess stand at left. Known as "Ironhead" during his Tarleton college days (1925–1929), Jess Davis was a two-sport (football and basketball), four-year letterman who played on seven state champion teams. In 1980, he received a spot in the Tarleton State University Athletic Hall of Fame. Pictured below, from left to right, George Sherrod, Welty Skipper, Henry Skipper, and Joe Parnell were on the Skipper's Gap baseball team, in a day when the nearest professional franchise—the St. Louis Cardinals, not the Texas Rangers—was the Erath County favorite. (Both, Marshall Sherrod.)

Some members of the Erath community punctuated their rural routine with games of chance. One such gathering is shown above being played outdoors on a blanket by members of the Cox and Little families. A starker contrast could hardly exist than the refined entertainment available to city and country dwellers on the northwest side of the square at Stephenville's Crow Opera House. Patronized by one of the wealthiest women in Erath County, the widow Mollie Jane Crow, this facility (below) provided surprisingly high-quality entertainment for an urban center so small and far removed from Texas's major population centers. Ever attuned to community needs, she left a sizable bequest that, in 1915, paid for the construction of the Mollie Crow Administration Building (later renamed Home Economics Building) on the John Tarleton College campus. (Above, Marshall Sherrod; below, Nancy Allen.)

Charter members of the Twentieth Century Club, organized in 1901, were, from left to right, Mrs. Hill Perry, Mrs. W. P. Orr, Mrs. Henry Mothershead, Mrs. C. O. Blakeny, Mrs. Ben Bassel, and Mrs. Collin George. Their efforts produced the Stephenville Public Library. Below, a less academic but, nonetheless, unique and interesting Stephenville novelty was the inimitable Ray's Gardens, which brought visitors from near and far. There, guests could view the often bizarre and unusual folk art of George Ellis Ray (1881–1957). He made sculptures of concrete, tile, colored glass, shells, and petrified rock. While visiting, guests could read Ray's homespun, thought-provoking, philosophical aphorisms, listening all the while to gospel music played through a loudspeaker system.

In the midst of the Great Depression, Stephenville's youth received a marvelous outlet for athletic energies and talent. The city's recreational hall came courtesy of Pres. Franklin Roosevelt's New Deal Works Progress Administration. Built between 1938 and 1939, near the end of the Depression, the facility provided (and still does today) a place where both adults and youngsters convened to play basketball almost every day of the week. The facility today sits on the northwest edge of Stephenville City Park, adjacent to a host of baseball and softball diamonds, outdoor basketball courts, and park benches and tables along the Bosque River. (Both, Debbie Cashell.)

Of late, the city's more popular diversions have ranged from the ridiculous to the sublime. Stephenville frequently hosts a wide array of activities and culinary delights on the Fourth of July in Stephenville City Park. At one point in recent history, armadillo races (above) were a genuine crowd pleaser, enjoyed by participants (probably not counting the armadillos) and spectators. Most recently, Splashville has become the newest recreational pride of the town. Located just inside the South Loop and in the southeast corner of City Park, this miniature water park, complete with its array of slides, waterfalls, lazy river, swimming lanes, comfortable lounge chairs, and colorful umbrellas, has something enjoyable for any water lover in town. (Below, Debbie Cashell.)

Seven

LOG SCHOOLHOUSES
TO SISD

As in most mid-19th-century Southern American frontier communities, Stephenville's earliest arrivals necessarily gave greater attention to nourishing and nurturing the body than the mind. Educating the community's young was, however, not entirely neglected. The small number of teachers (12) and students (46) in the 1860 federal population census betrays the rudimentary nature of Erath County education. But those figures do not mean that county residents failed to recognize the fundamental need to properly educate Stephenville's youth. The city's first primitive schoolhouse was apparently a log cabin, off the southeast corner of the square, a structure also used by the Masons and for church services. By the mid-1870s, a tuition school called Stephenville College included the first grade through college and convened in a two-story stone building on Paddock Street.

The images in this chapter reveal the dramatic development of public education in Stephenville over a century and a half. From early, simple one-room schoolhouses, scattered across Erath County's landscape, there has evolved a sophisticated, well-developed Stephenville Independent School District (SISD), capable of cultivating both the body and mind. As in earliest days, instruction in "readin', ritin', and 'rithmatic" remains, but each successive generation of Stephenville educators has added to these fundamentals a variety of robust programs producing National Merit Scholars, Texas Education Agency (TEA)–certified exemplary schools at the elementary and secondary levels, and a corps of individual and team championships at both the district and state levels in University Interscholastic League (UIL) academics and athletics. The trophy cases of SISD schools burgeon with hardware richly documenting successes at every level and in every activity of public education.

The journey has been one from country school kids, often with only the basic necessities of life, to youthful champions triumphantly holding their awards atop the winner's stand. Photographs taken along the way portray the tale. Chapter seven provides revealing glimpses of this unfolding process and the rise of public education as one of the most important and determining elements in the lives of Stephenville children, young and old.

At the turn of the 20th century, Harry McIlhaney, son of the Stephenville College president Dr. Marshall McIlhaney, opened McIlhaney Academy. It was a two-story structure in the northern part of town that was located somewhat west of today's Clinton and Vanderbilt Streets. The tuition school had three teachers and about 100 students. McIlhaney Academy, shown below in 1911, closed its doors in 1916 due to lack of finances. At the public school level, the SHS graduating class of 1906 (above) included, from left to right, (first row) Sue Jett Cherry and unidentified; (second row) W. Gaston, Jack Reil, Kit Bridges, and Oran Ferguson. By 1919, the senior class had grown to 19 members.

Above is the Stephenville public school constructed at the intersection of Paddock and College Streets in the 1870s. By the time this photograph was taken in 1908, not long before the building's demolition, this facility had become too small to provide the needs for all the school-aged children in the city. As the number of students grew during the early 20th century, Stephenville sorely needed a new public school facility. The firm Holderness and Oates built a three-story structure that was christened Central Ward School. After completion of the full cement basement, the builders laid the cornerstone at the November 28, 1907, public dedication ceremony, shown below. Nona Laney Ferguson, Ludie Frank Mills, Edith Jones Disharoon, and one unidentified pose for the picture in the buggy. (Below, CTHI:DSLC.)

HIGH SCHOOL, STEPHENVILLE, TEXAS   From Perry Bros., Druggists

The finished brick building (above), completed in March 1908, included 18 large classrooms, a spacious third-floor auditorium, and a stylish bell tower and was heated by a wood-burning stove. Central Ward School served as Stephenville's only school until the early 1920s, when it became a primary school after the construction of a new Stephenville High School building. In 1921, this new high school (at left) began serving the educational needs of Stephenville's increasing teenage population. (Above, Wayne Sherrod; at left, Marshall Sherrod.)

Education occurred both in and outside the classroom. Above, in the early 1950s, a group of Stephenville public school elementary students pose on a field trip in front of the "Rec Hall." However, not every early-20th-century Erath County student came to town for education. Below, teacher Sam Russell (1889–1971) is shown 13 miles east of town in 1917 with some of his students at Johnsville Rural School. After World War I, Russell practiced law and served as county attorney (1919–1924), district attorney (1924–1928), judge for the 29th Judicial District (1928–1940), and U.S. representative from Texas's 17th District (1941–1947). (Above, Debbie Cashell; below, Marshall Sherrod.)

One- or two-room schoolhouses provided the first through the eighth grades for children living in Stephenville's hinterland. Two such groups of students attending Marathal Gap in 1923 (above) and Johnsville Rural School in 1929 (below) are shown here. The former posed outside the school building and the latter in their classroom. By the late 1930s, SHS had grown. The Yellow Jackets are now its mascot and it sports school colors of blue and gold. Depending on the year, the senior class numbered more than 70 but less than 199. The school had between 13 and 16 teachers. The growing SHS student body in part reflected an effective busing system that brought students to town from Chalk Mountain, Johnsville, Bluff Dale, and Selden to complete their high school education at SHS. (Both, Marshall Sherrod.)

First-year educator Marshal Sherrod (first row, center) served as principal and teacher for the fifth through the eighth grades at the two-room Johnsville Rural School (1941–1942). His first assignment was to paint the old school building by himself before school started. The student body that academic year numbered 30. The facility (now consolidated with Pony Creek and Chalk Mountain) operates today as Three-Way School, and SISD has absorbed most students living in nearby outlying areas of Erath County. Sherrod's 1941–1942 Johnsville teaching contract (below) yielded $780, which is $10,300 in today's economy. Happily, the pay scale has improved. The state minimum salary schedule for a starting teacher in 2010–2011 is $27,320. (Both, Marshall Sherrod.)

In a day before stringent eligibility requirements, sturdy teenage farm boys attracted the attention of Stephenville High School coaches who built their athletic programs by helping promising prospects move to town. There, these lads could contribute, along with athletic city boys, to the SHS sports program. As early as 1911, SHS athletes received sideline and courtside support from "Yell Leaders" like the group shown below. By 1937, the uniforms had evolved (above), but for many years, both boys and girls were part of the high school cheerleading squad. Pictured above, from left to right, are Lois Latham, Gordon Hill, Virginia Wolfe, and Grady Daniels. Gender equality lasted, at least off and on, through the 1940s. (Above, Marshall Sherrod; below, Debbie Cashell.)

Other traditions that survive and thrive today include the bee mascot (shown at right in 1977) and the award-winning dance performance team, the SHS Stingerettes (below). Created in 1953, in those early days all members of the "Stings" carried batons. More recently, the batons have fallen by the wayside, but the dance team annually brings home its own share of trophies from state-level competitions. The SHS Vocational Building on the east side of campus proudly displays a sign proclaiming the Stingerettes as "Grand Champions in Dance." (At right, Debbie Cashell.)

Little sailor middies and dark stockings were part of the 1911 SHS girls basketball team uniforms (above). By the 1920s, the girls team was quite successful, although none achieved the heights reached by the 1968 Honey Bees who won the 3A Girls State Basketball title, with the final score of 39-27 over West Orange (below). Coach Sam Taylor's 1968 Honey Bees brought the first high school state-level athletic team title to Stephenville. Until 1979, girls basketball was played half-court, rather than full. In the broad sweep of SHS girls basketball history since 1955, Honey Bee teams have made the playoffs 39 times and brought home 29 district championships. (Above, Debbie Cashell; below, SISD.)

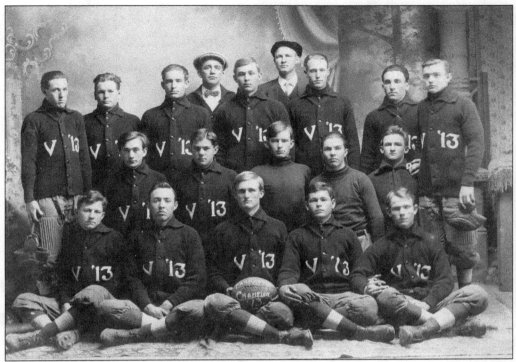

Although some dispute the date of the earliest SHS football team, the picture above suggests the football program began no later than 1913. By 1923, the team improved enough to make the state semifinals. In 1930, SHS won the district championship under the leadership of head coach Joe Brown, who coached from 1926 to 1933, with a record 30-25-7, and assistant coach Jim Mobley. Below in the back row, fourth from left, is Hugh Wolfe, who would go on to play at Tarleton Junior College and then University of Texas where, in the summer of 1938, he became that school's first NFL draft pick. Wolfe later played fullback for the 1938 NFL champions, the New York Giants. (Above, Debbie Cashell.)

Coach Brown brought a District 12 championship to Stephenville in his final year (1933). Three years later, Jim Mobley assumed head coaching duties. During his two-year tenure (1936–1937), Mobley went 18-1-0, compiling the highest win percentage—0.947—of any coach in Yellow Jacket history. His 1937 team appears above. Mobley's accomplishments prefigured the four state titles collected by SHS in the 1990s, as well as the football mania that characterizes Stephenville still today. While SHS enjoyed occasional football success over the next half-century—particularly a 1953 quarter-final appearance directed by quarterback (and later Fort Worth *Star-Telegram* columnist) Jerry Flemmons—it was not until the 1988 arrival of Art Briles, shown in his office below in 1998, that the Yellow Jackets became a perennial Texas football power. (Above, Marshall Sherrod; below, author.)

During his 12 seasons (1988–1999) directing Yellow Jacket football, Briles compiled a 136-29-2 record and forever changed Stephenville's self-image. Since 1989, the Yellow Jackets have made the playoffs 21 seasons. During the fall, Friday nights witness an exodus of multiple thousands from town to all away games. Meanwhile, Friday mornings drew large crowds for *Coffee With Coach*, a 93.1 KSTV half-hour radio program hosted by the "Voice of the Yellow Jackets," Boots Elliott. Shown above, Elliott interviews Briles during the 1999 playoff season. Shown below in the giddy aftermath of the 1998 4A Division II state championship game, Briles and team celebrate the 34-7 victory over La Marque that brought the Yellow Jackets' single season yardage total to 8,664, breaking the national high school record. (Above, author; below, Fort Worth *Star-Telegram*.)

During the Briles era, SHS won 4A state titles in 1993, 1994, 1998, and 1999, prompting many Texas football sportswriters to deem the 1990s an SHS "Decade of Dominance." Dublin's Dr. Pepper bottling plant, located 15 miles southwest of Stephenville, celebrated each championship with commemorative collector's item cans. SHS coaches and players earned state rings (above). Meanwhile, a local 1998 "Got Milk" billboard combined two Stephenville passions—dairy and football—featuring wide receiver Cody Cardwell, linebacker Jack Hodges (who played the entire championship game with a heavily braced broken ankle), and quarterback Kelan Luker sporting milk mustaches. Luker's 4,700 yards became the state single-season passing yardage mark. Cardwell's single-season 2,427 receiving yards was the national high school record through 2008. His 4,241 career receiving yards remained a Texas record until Jordan Shipley broke it in 2003. (Above, Debbie Cashell; below, author.)

The Briles era also brought the "Can Fan" to Texas schoolboy football. Often distressing opposing teams and fans, hundreds of can fans attend every game carrying metal ball bearing–filled containers ranging from hand-held vessels to butane tanks and even the massive adapted oil drum shown above. From pre-game drills to the final gun, Yellow Jacket fans shake their cans at every game. Below, KC and TJ Steed hold super-can "Big Bertha," created for the 1999 state championship. As a preteen, TJ along with his dad, Dr. Steve Steed of TSU, invented the concept that has become intertwined with the community's involvement in the football program. Eleven days before the 1999 final, *Dallas Morning News* sportswriter John Marshall appropriately dubbed SHS "Quarterback High" in his article "Stephenville Legacy: Yellow Jackets dominate '90s with top QBs." (Above, Debbie Cashell; below, Heather Steed.)

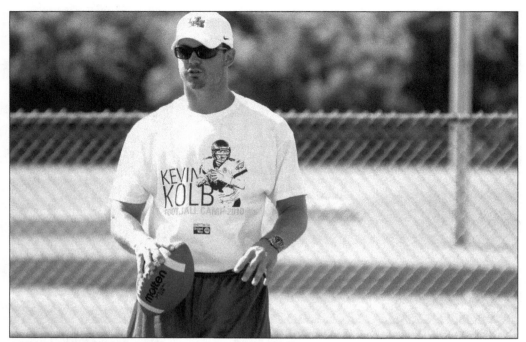

Signal callers Branndon Stewart (1993) and Glenn Odell (1994) brought Stephenville its first back-to-back state titles; Kelan Luker (1998) and Kendal Briles (1999) brought its second pair. Subsequent field generals have made their mark as well. Above, Kevin Kolb (1999–2002) enjoyed conspicuous success at SHS and University of Houston (where this four-year starter's 12,964 passing yards ranked him fifth on the NCAA Division 1-A all-time list). Kolb returns regularly to Stephenville, where (above) he conducts a summer football camp. In April 2010, the Philadelphia Eagles announced Kolb as their season starter. In a closely fought 2005 4A state semifinal, billed locally as "Flannel Shirts vs. Plaid Skirts," *Parade* magazine, and Army High School All-American Jevan Snead led the Yellow Jackets against the Highland Park Scots. Snead appears at left with head coach Chad Morris, who coached from 2003 to 2007 with a record of 49-10. (Above, Debbie Cashell; at left, author.)

Head coaches Mike Copeland, who coached from 2000 to 2002 with a record of 26-9, and Joseph Gillespie, from 2008 to the present with a record of 27-13, continue to perpetuate the football championship tradition. Meanwhile, the athletic successes have by no means been limited to pigskin play. Power lifting began as an SHS sport in 1989. SHS won the Division 1 Texas High School Power Lifting Association state championship in 2001. Team members pictured below are, from left to right, (first row) Jerrod Elliot, Justin Monk, Cory Henderson, Jonathan Miller, and Pedro Medina; (second row) Tye Gunn, head coach Randy Clements, coach Joseph Gillespie, and coach Robbie Tindol. Monk won the individual 2001 state title in the 165-pound weight class. (Above, Debbie Cashell; below, SISD.)

In 2006, Cheyne Stephen, a descendant of pioneer William Franklin Stephen, achieved Texas power-lifting immortality by winning his fourth consecutive individual state championship. Between 2003 and 2006, Stephen gathered his titles in three different weight classes (114.5, 123.5, and 132.5 pounds, respectively). Not to be left behind, Honey Bee athletics has built a winning volleyball tradition since the introduction of the program in the 1960s. In addition to making 13 trips to the playoffs through 2010, the 2003 team below won the 4A state championship in San Marcos, defeating Highland Park 26-24, 25-15, and 25-19. (At left, Neal Stephen; below, SISD.)

SHS academic accolades also abound. Building on the work of Stanley Miller, a longtime science and math teacher, UIL academic coordinator, and namesake of the science wing, SHS has greatly excelled. UIL state champion coaches are, from left to right, (first row) Vickie Amos (Poetry, 2009) and Jan Vaughn (Accounting, 1991); (second row) Lise Schwartzkopf (Current Issues and Events [CI&E], 2006 and 2007), Brenda Burks (Spelling and Vocabulary, 2001), and Annette Pierce Sherrod (Literary Criticism, 1998, 2001, 2003, and 2007). Appropriately, Miller was among the inaugural 2005 inductees in the SHS Academic Hall of Fame. Below, six-time state 4A UIL medalist, 2007 CI&E individual state champion, and National Merit Scholar Finalist Brandon Ratliff (far right) appears with his second place state CI&E team members, from left to right, Samantha Parsons, Clint Doty, and Caleb Graves. (Above, Debbie Cashell; below, author.)

Considering Erath County's rural economy, it is not surprising that agricultural education has flourished at SHS. First mention of an SHS Agricultural Club and Stock Judging Team appears in 1922. The SHS chapter of FFA began in the 1940s and rapidly expanded during the following decade. SHS's first FFA state president took office in 1970. In recent years, SHS has received national attention when Alyssa Spruill (left) and Sarah Wolf won first place at the 2008 National FFA Agriscience Fair at the National FFA Convention. More recently, Sabrina Huston, DeWayne Phillips, Matt Willis, and Aron Hutchins (shown below from left to right) won a national title in meat judging at the 2009 Western National Roundup. (Both, Laurah Williams.)

In 2008, multiple Erath County UFO sightings received national publicity on everything from *Larry King Live* to *Late Night with David Letterman*. It also prompted visits to Stephenville from the Mutual UFO Network. The SHS Science Club, first founded in 1941 and resurrected in recent years, approached the sightings in a jocular, skeptical spirit, making over $6,000 in scholarship funds. The money came from the sale of 1,800 "Here for the Milk" T-shirts, which are modeled above, from left to right, by Kelley Royal, Kenzie Paschal, and Alex Huckabee. At right, Ben Gilbert is congratulated by neighbor Evelyn Pierce at the 2000 dedication of Gilbert Elementary School. During his productive tenure (1956–1995), Gilbert served as SHS agriculture teacher, assistant principal and counselor, principal, SISD assistant superintendent, and superintendent. (Above, Kathleen Huckabee; at right, author.)

Academic excellence has become an SISD hallmark because of exceptional instructional leadership. The SISD School Board was one of only five boards selected for Texas 2007 Honor School Boards, a distinction conferred by the Texas Association of School Administrators in Austin. In the above photograph, board president Dr. Ann Calahan is third from left in the first row, and superintendent Dr. Darrell Floyd is on the far right in the second row. The board also received recognition as the 2007 Educational Service Center Region XI School Board of the Year. Below, the SHS faculty displays their 2009–2010 Exemplary banner for meeting the highest Texas Education Agency standards for student classroom performance. SHS was the only 4A Region XI high school to receive exemplary status and was one of only 13—the top five percent—in Texas Conference 4A. (Above, SISD; below, www.jonesfamilyphotography.com.)

Eight

TARLETON STATE

As John Tarleton neared the end of his life in 1895, he disliked both Stephenville and its residents. His antipathy sprang from a disagreement with a Stephenville tax collector over property taxes. This dispute nearly cost Stephenville College, closed in 1895, the $85,000 endowment that ultimately revived the town's earliest institution of higher learning. Tarleton's Stephenville attorney J. C. George prevailed upon the aging merchant-rancher to change his mind.

Tarleton's bequest resulted in the 1899 founding of John Tarleton College. Eight years later, it became a junior college. In 1917, House Bill No. 598 made Tarleton a coeducational part of Texas A&M's system, rechristening it John Tarleton Agricultural College. The name changed again in 1949 to Tarleton State College. In 1959, Tarleton once more became a four-year college, granting its first bachelors' degrees in 1963. Among its prestigious graduates of the 1960s were Bob Glasgow (1966 student body president, former Texas state senator, and attorney in the Stephenville firm Glasgow Taylor Isham Glasgow) and Mike Moncrief (1967 student body president, former Texas state senator and Tarrant County judge, and today's Fort Worth mayor). Well-known Western artist Kenneth Wyatt also attended Tarleton. In 1972, Tarleton introduced a master's degree program. Finally, in 1973, the name changed to today's Tarleton State University.

During its early history, Tarleton specialized in quality education in agriculture, home economics, and military training. In 1921, it introduced the Reserve Officer Training Corps (ROTC) and courses in military science and tactics. As World War II approached, Tarleton's ROTC became one of America's foremost training grounds for soldiers in the making, bound for war. Between 1917 (when Tarleton became a state institution) and 1943, Tarleton provided education for 12,000 students. Postwar enrollment expanded dramatically, exceeding 3,000 annually during the 1970s and reaching more than 6,000 students, served by 200 faculty members, during the 1990s. A 1,200-acre ranch complements today's 165-acre campus. Historically, the TSU rodeo, basketball, football, and track programs have performed well at the national level. With modern facilities and a 21st-century enrollment of over 9,000, Tarleton's future looks bright.

JOHN TARLETON

A MEMORIAL TO
THE FOUNDER OF

TARLETON COLLEGE

May 1, 1933   Stephenville, Texas

The pamphlet at left, published in 1933, was for Parents' Day and Tarleton Memorial Service on April 29–30, 1928. It preserves the program and speeches honoring the benefactor whose bequest made today's Tarleton State University possible. Founder's Day, itself, has a long history dating from 1902. Below, the first Tarleton students pay respect to the man whose donation breathed life into the defunct Stephenville College, reviving the institution on which today's Tarleton State University was built. (Both, CTHI:DSLC.)

J. C. George was a partner in the Stephenville law firm of Martin and George. He represented John Tarleton in a lawsuit, in which Tarleton was accused as plaintiff for violation of the Anti-herd Law. George so impressed Tarleton with his management of the suit that the aging rancher transferred all his legal business from Weatherford to George's care in Stephenville, including the crafting of Tarleton's final will. Below, students pose before the impressive gothic structure that served as Tarleton's first facility. This building was at the northwest corner of today's Tarleton and McIlhaney Streets, which is where a gazebo stands today. (Both, CTHI:DSLC.)

The first director and president of struggling Stephenville College (1893–1895) was Marshall McIlhaney. After Tarleton's $85,000 endowment came to the rescue, Erath County Judge Thomas B. King (at left) became embroiled in an 1896–1899 power struggle over control of the new college with Texas governor Charles Allen Culberson. Their differences included disagreement over the college mission and whether McIlhaney should remain college president. Culberson eventually won, and in September 1899, W. H. Bruce received appointment as John Tarleton College's new president. Edgar Elliot Bramlette became president in 1900. His wife, Louise Linn Bramlette (below), was a charter member and first president of the Twentieth Century Club. The book reception she organized in 1902 was the largest social gathering ever held in Stephenville. The function brought 250 books to the college library. (Both, CTHI:DSLC.)

The course and character of Tarleton as an institution has been greatly shaped by its many chief administrators. James F. Cox (at right) served in that role for six years (1913–1919). He proposed offering the institution to Texas A&M as a branch campus, a proposal accepted in September 1917. J. Thomas Davis (below) followed Cox, serving from 1919–1945, the longest tenure of any chief executive officer at the school. Davis recruited talented faculty, oversaw a dramatic expansion and renovation of the college physical plant, and raised the visibility of Tarleton to both the state and national levels. During the Davis years, Tarleton had a preparatory division for junior and senior high school students and a college division for freshmen and sophomore college students. The high school division endured until Davis's 1945 retirement. (Both, CTHI:DSLC.)

Street View, Leading to John Tarlton College, Stephenville, Texas

Pub. for R. E. Cox   *Where Gilbert will go this year.*

In 1908, Bosque (now Tarleton) Street above, leading to Tarleton's campus, bore faint resemblance to the thoroughfare existing today. One of the most memorable campus landmarks in those days was the East Gate, shown below, with cadets assembled at the entryway of Military Drive. Tarleton's landmark rock walls and gates were typically gifts from graduating classes. (Both, CTHI:DSLC.)

Another early Tarleton landmark was the "dog house," a small wooden structure around a well, erected by the college to serve as a male bathhouse. Shown above in 1905, a water tower surmounted this 12-by-18-foot green wooden edifice. There, male students could shower and change clothes. Three years later, a group of Tarleton coeds posed in front of the Mary Corn Wilkerson Dormitory (at right), constructed from Thurber brick. This was the third building on Tarleton's campus. (Both, CTHI:DSLC.)

The 1920 Tarleton graduating class, shown above, numbered just over 130 students, not quite a quarter of the entire student body. Enrollment for the 1919–1920 school year

At the turn of the century, cultural outlets and opportunities for self-development were readily available to Tarleton students. The 1905 Alethea Club was a literary society for coeds who systematically studied the lives and literature of various authors. Club members also devoted themselves to music, recitations, and debate. (CTHI:DSLC.)

was 611. The class of 1920 helped launch the college newspaper *J-TAC*. (CTHI:DSLC.)

During 1905, this group of Tarleton coeds improved speaking skills through enrollment in Tarleton's speech class. (CTHI:DSLC.)

The intellectual center of any university is the library. Lula P. Martin, pictured above in the 1920s, was the first college librarian and manager of the college store. In the mid–20th century, Tarleton made a huge leap forward, opening a new and modern library building, which still serves its students today. Over 1,000 people, including Chancellor M. T. Harrington of the Texas A&M College System, attended the November 1956 dedication of the library facility (below). (Both, CTHI:DSLC.)

Inside Tarleton's library, employees pose at the new circulation counter that was donated by the 1939 senior class. Above, standing second from the left is Dick Smith. In March 1974, the library (at right) was named in his honor. Smith taught at Tarleton from 1933 through 1973. A Harvard doctor of philosophy, he served as head of the Department of Social Sciences from 1948 to 1967 and was known for his high expectations of students and colleagues, his richly informative lectures, and his scholarly publications. Smith left most of his wealth to the university. That legacy benefits students today in the form of coveted "Dick Smith Scholarships." (Both, CTHI:DSLC.)

While ROTC was officially introduced in the fall of 1921, Tarleton's cadet corps and its military tradition existed from the institution's founding. Above, the cadet corps of 1904–1905 pose for a group photograph. A Student Army Training Corps was established in the fall of 1918 to allow students to receive schooling and military training simultaneously. Tarleton's precision ROTC drill team, the Wainwright Rifles, first appeared on April 13, 1949. Named for Gen. Jonathan Matthew Wainwright, U.S. commander in the Philippine Islands during World War II, the unit performed at many prestigious venues. The drill team's finest hour came on January 20, 1961, when it marched in the JFK inauguration parade. (Both, CTHI:DSLC.)

The Tarleton cadet corps (above) helped to produce one of the war's best-known heroes, Lt. Col. William Dyess. He attended Tarleton as a pre-law major (1934–1936) and later served with distinction in the Pacific Theater of Operations. During that worldwide conflict, George Kennedy (1967 Academy Award winner of Best Supporting Actor in *Cool Hand Luke*) came to Stephenville in July 1943 as part of the Army Specialized Training Program. Through intensive study, the ASTP provided army officers a vast array of technical training. Tarleton was one of many colleges and universities across America specially selected as a suitable site for this purpose. Kennedy returned to Tarleton in both 1969 and 1981. He is pictured below on one of those visits with local notables. From left to right they are George Kennedy, unidentified, Ernie Wolfe, and Hugh Wolfe. (Both, CTHI:DSLC.)

Regularly scheduled athletic contests began in 1904, when Tarleton entered the West Texas College League. Its 1905 football team (above) captured the league title. In later years, William J. Wisdom (at left) became one of Tarleton's most successful football coaches, compiling a career record of 71-35-15. He took his 1925 Plowboys to an 8-0-1 record and the state junior college championship. That team outscored opponents 276-25. In 1930, Wisdom added head basketball coach to his duties, inheriting a program that had won state championships in 1917, 1926, 1928, and 1929. (Both, CTHI:DSLC.)

William J. Wisdom successfully learned the sport of basketball. Between 1934 and 1938, he coached his teams to "The Streak," 86 consecutive wins, which was not surpassed in college basketball until UCLA's immortal John Wooden's Bruins did it in 1974. Wisdom's 1935 team appears above. They are, from left to right, coach Wisdom, Arthur Torvie, Vernon Payne, Cortez Killen, Jude Smith, Oran Spears, Elmer Finley, James Britt, Jim Carrigan, Willie Tate, and Joe Headstream. On February 26, 1972, Tarleton named its basketball facility Wisdom Gym. Recently, both men's and women's basketball fortunes have revived. Jan Lowery's 1991–1992 team went 30-8, earning a trip to the NAIA National Tournament, where the TexAnns lost the championship game 73-56 to the State College of South Dakota. Meanwhile, in the championship tradition of Wisdom's teams of the 1930s, Lonn Reisman (pictured below in the center of the second row) took his 2005 team to the NCAA Division II Final Four. (Above, CTHI:DSLC; below, TSU Sports Information.)

In April 1926, Stephenville residents exhumed John Tarleton's body (originally placed in Mount Pisgah Cemetery at Patillo), reinterring his remains, under the cover of darkness, on the Tarleton campus. A second removal became necessary, as the college expanded its boundaries. Today John Tarleton rests at the west-southwest corner of the TSU campus in Tarleton Park, beneath an obelisk (at left), just south of Washington Street and adjacent to the West End Cemetery. On October 10, 1987, the State of Texas honored Tarleton's legacy by placing a historical marker (below) beside his monument. (Both, Debbie Cashell.)

Nine

MAKIN' MUSIC

In the minds of most Americans, the melodies and words of high school or college fight songs and alma maters are often just beneath the conscious surface. Although this volume provides sights, not sounds, it nevertheless offers a glimpse at the music makers who have entertained and delighted Stephenville residents and music lovers across the 20th and 21st centuries.

Graduates of SHS and Tarleton are beholden to the bands and choirs that acquainted Stephenville with the now familiar songs performed at pep rallies, bonfires, athletic contests, graduation exercises, concerts, church assemblies, and a score of other venues. SHS has produced professional musicians Barney McCollum (bass trombonist who played with "The President's Own" Marine Corps band in Washington); Phil O'Banion (Temple University Boyer College of Music and Dance lecturer in percussion); Gary Whitman (Texas Christian University professor of clarinet and Fort Worth Symphony member); and John Lane (Sam Houston State University faculty assistant professor of percussion). TSU hosts an annual Tarleton Jazz Festival, and has brought Maynard Ferguson, the Count Basie Orchestra, David "Fathead" Newman, and many others to town.

Stephenville's musical heritage is not limited, however, to the melodies and songs of educational or religious institutions. The city's residents have delighted in the country and western songs of local talent performing at the Cross Timbers Opry, which was established in 1979, and better-known performers on the stage of City Limits. Some are local notables, donating time and effort to their passion. Others have more recognizable names with hit records and a national or international following. Four celebrated recording artists—Jewel, Larry Joe Taylor, Lee Roy Parnell, and Johnny Duncan—have considered Stephenville home. City Limits and the open-air Birdsong Amphitheater in Stephenville City Park frequently host visits from popular performers like Pat Green, Cory Morrow, Charlie Robison, Kevin Fowler, Gary P. Nunn, Davin James, Asleep at the Wheel, the Cody Gill Band, and the Randy Rogers Band. Meanwhile, the Glenn Miller Orchestra and Fort Worth Symphony also have performed at Birdsong.

In the early 20th century, a wide variety of musical forms were found in Erath County. The 1904 Johnson Schoolhouse Fiddle Band dressed the patriot part, posing above with their various instruments. Pictured below, 11 Tarleton coeds in a 1909 piano class sit for a group photograph.

Hired by Dean Davis in 1919, Dennis G. Hunewell (at right) served as Tarleton's band director for 22 years. During that time, he built the Tarleton Military Band, a first-class musical performing group that was extensively used across Texas to raise Tarleton's visibility and attract enrollment of quality students. Acting as ambassadors of the college, the band (below) traveled across Texas raising awareness about Tarleton as a good place to secure a college education. (Both, CTHI:DSLC)

In 1928, Hunewell Bandstand was completed as a gift from the classes of 1926–1928. A Tarleton band poses in front of the bandstand above. Music at Tarleton also came courtesy of a college dance band. Shown below, a 1941–1942 group of 10 musicians, led by future Stephenville mayor J. Louis Evans (second row, third from left) and vocalist Lettye Warden, prepare for a performance. (Both, CTHI:DSLC.)

Tarleton was not the only Stephenville educational institution supporting a band. In 1936, SHS organized its first band under director T. P. Craddock. Only 6 of its 40 members had previous musical training. The band played for assemblies and graduation. Two years later, a dapper SHS band appears above on the school steps, smartly outfitted in uniforms, holding instruments, and ready to perform. Below, the SHS band lines up in marching formation adjacent to the high school.

In fact, the SHS chorus, introduced in 1921, predated the creation of the Yellow Jacket Band. Choral groups proved quite popular at the high school. In 1970, three SHS students made the All-State Choir. In 1974, that number rose to four. More recently, Titus Wamala made All-State Choir in back-to-back years (2006–2007), as did Amanda Kirby (2009–2010). After her second selection to the All-State Women's Choir, Amanda (far right) stands, from left to right, with her father, Jim; SHS choir director John Tucker; and her mother, Anita. Music has proven equally popular in Stephenville outside the boundaries of public and collegiate education. Below, Birdsong Theater in Stephenville City Park provides a popular venue for free public concerts. On a regular basis, an eclectic assortment of Birdsong's performers brings large crowds to City Park. (Above, John Tucker; below, Debbie Cashell.)

Among the frequent guests at the Texstar Ford Summer Nights Concert Series is the Western swing group, Asleep at the Wheel. Above, Ray Benson (left) and the group entertain the large crowd that regularly gathers on the grassy slope leading down to the Birdsong Theater. Below, the world of music and rodeo united when three-time Grammy nominee and singing star Jewel and nine-time world champion cowboy Ty Murray married in August 2008. (Above, *Empire-Tribune*; below, Joe Hardwick.)

Songwriter, singer, and recording artist Larry Joe Taylor (at left) is a much-loved musician among Stephenville's music fans. His popularity is amplified by the Larry Joe Taylor's Texas Music Festival and Chili Cook-off, which is now over two decades old. These annual festivities take place at the 380-acre Melody Mountain Ranch, located 5 miles north of Stephenville. The event draws crowds of 30,000 or more and has been named as one of the four top Texas music festivals by *Performing Songwriter* magazine. Taylor's music reveals his passion for life along the halcyon Texas ("Third") Coast and in the Caribbean Islands. (Both, www. larryjoetaylor.com/media.htm.)

ABOUT THE ORGANIZATION

The Stephenville Museum provides unique opportunities to touch the past. Founded in 1966 to preserve the history of the Cross Timbers region, the museum has attracted donations from area founding families.

The 1869 Gothic-style limestone Berry Cottage anchors the property. The grounds feature over a dozen historic buildings, including several log cabins and outbuildings, a ranch house, a two-room schoolhouse, a blacksmith shop, and a chapel. In 2010, a Queen Anne–style, Oxford residence was donated to the museum. This two-story structure will be moved to a site on the museum grounds.

The museum is a busy place year-round. Tours are available daily, with the grounds forming a well-recognized backdrop for area photographers. Weddings in the romantic Chapel on the Bosque are intimate affairs, with guests seated on original curved pews, in the glow of the restored stained glass windows. Meetings, reunions, and receptions are hosted in the Center Grove School and in the outdoor spaces. The Bosque River Walk links the museum to foot and bicycle traffic between downtown and Stephenville City Park.

Annual public events bring throngs of visitors onto the museum property. In the spring, an Heirloom Plant Fair features local vendors with native and heirloom specimens. During early summer, Camp Pioneer teaches children about life long ago. Each October, By-Gone Days on the Bosque is a full-blown salute to the past. Reenactors, traditional craftsmen, and country music team up to entertain and educate guests.

Thousands of artifacts, documents, and photographs make up the museum's permanent collection. The structures on the grounds provide a perfect setting for displaying the period furniture and objects from the collection. Photographs, like the ones featured in this book, are stored in the museum's archives, with other documents and research materials.

Come celebrate the past at the Stephenville Museum. To learn more about the museum collection and events, visit the Stephenville Museum on the Internet at www.stephenville.com/museum.

Stephenville Museum
525 E. Washington Street
Stephenville, Texas 76401
(254) 965-5880
svillemuseum@embarqmail.com

Visit us at
arcadiapublishing.com

....

Printed in the USA
CPSIA information can be obtained
at www.ICGtesting.com
LVHW071024211223
766685LV00056B/919